IMBOLG

Máighréad Medbh

IMBOLG

ARLEN
HOUSE

Imbolg

is published in 2020 by
ARLEN HOUSE
42 Grange Abbey Road
Baldoyle, Dublin 13, Ireland
Phone: 00 353 86 8360236
info@arlenhouse.ie
www.arlenhouse.ie

978–1–85132–247–3, *paperback*

Distributed internationally by
SYRACUSE UNIVERSITY PRESS
621 Skytop Road, Suite 110
Syracuse, NY 13244–5290
Phone: 315–443–5534
Fax: 315–443–5545
supress@syr.edu
syracuseuniversitypress.syr.edu

poems © Máighréad Medbh, 2020

Typesetting by Arlen House

cover image:
Photograph by Monika Reder
http://monikarederphotography.com

CONTENTS

IMBOLG

PART I

IMBOLG

A new season
My mother's wintered womb, goodbye.
It hasn't been an easy passage, sea unquiet
in a pitch of murky shots and shockings.
Take and eat me, Glut of Light, display me
in your bare-arsed honesty. Here I come
breaching the small gap like a spear
        hand and leg before me.
She screams.
I am her pain.

Inside her everywhere I met a challenge.
Wall became wall of mirrors, faces I couldn't read.
And not a shred of scent to tell me was I
ram or ewe or what but a hard desire.
Rampant, ringed by stares, I bucked
butted, smashed my image, gashed myself
        got hooked on sheer fight.
She broke.
Toppled my home.

Now who's the lamb. I raise my chin
and wail once for the lost season, a blasted waste.
But no regret. I never planned the wreckage.
Or the slicing spear. I claim innocence.
Her body started it not mine.
However much she hates me I must stand
        upon my splayed limbs
and learn
to bound.

Begin
Begin always, a poet said, but how.
Californians and Shamans erase history –
or so they claim – slow thought to a wide motion.
Begin again and die.
The man believed his scuppered prostate cursed.
The woman's lymph declined.
Marisa left the convent chasing sex and family –
innocent, deceived, succumbed to uterine cancer.
By forty-five the clock wound down.

Land ahoy and there's the heart to jump and run
shivered in the lower deck, jaded by what it's been.
Scan the Heart find a picture in the Brain.
Scan the Brain find History and the lie of Substance.
I've repeated in the close night that the past
is its own self and I an other,
fought the dark theme that steals the show.
You, it goes, *You Judas. Hang.*

Vista
The window has entered a merger with air.
Out now in the perilous street and not
mouse among the purposed volutions but
one of them, knowing why each foot follows
the other, engined by a lithic rationale.
That graceful building taller than the rest –
the one with the compound sunglasses –
that's my goal.
A map in my head, I deftly weave
round blinkered cars across the ten-lane torrent.
Fly-leap the dashed lines.
Bond. Batman. Spidey.
Why wait when you know where you're going.

Sosafe

I wouldn't, she says, spine winged by the floral sofa.
She glances curiously towards the netted window
and notes the weird hat of a random passer.
One promise. One track. One daily remade bed.

She thought herself big once,
a bucking thing no rule could ride.
Her astrolabe snagged on Jupiter's moons
who burned their pennyeach into her palms.

Once the wedding dress had tucked its neck
into its snowy breast, she became gangly legs
and played housewitch. Walls thickened.
She no nucleus but essential organelle.

Now embedded in the structure it's her umbrella.
Boy it's wet beyond. This Life and its Weathers.
I am virtuous, she tells herself, *I honour my contracts.*
Come rain hail or sudden fire, I hold to the ship.

when this postless bed is shared by someone so
uncertain of my worth. I mean, my father held
my hand as though its every phalanx were aglow
with jewels that needed to be hourly honed.
Spoiled – like a cake, or a spirit improperly distilled?
I think not. I mean, I never had designer dresses
or a car, but overlarge hips and several stresses.

I can't abide women without grace and poise;
or rather, I consider them my abject foils.
I don't ask to be waited on, much as I'd enjoy
a lady's maid to brush my hair and coil
it into small snakes. I could become embroiled
in the commonalty but I make sure I'm set apart.
Hold to my family, flaunt my man, curt my heart.

What work am I supposed to do? Believe me it's pain
to be dependent. The title is his, though my way is regal
and I administer with great efficiency this small domain.
My eyes were on a posied dream, some high-as-an-eagle
notion, when I cut short my career and made a personal
commitment that seemed much more. Paradise decision
it was then, but time is both execution and inquisition.

I still dream of gems and fine dresses. I follow the royals,
watch *Desperate Housewives*, wonder why he doesn't see
the value in a simply devoted wife. He goes out, disloyal
probably, but I don't dwell on that. I settle on my routine
and map my hours in orbits round this limited scene.
I make sure that every task is plotted and complete.
For fear of usurpation, I'm silent as a starched sheet.

PALE GLOBE

The ball is what she has.
Long threads made spare from winding.
In it she has bound and cloned his ways,
his methods, all their moments, little habits

knit in teguments, offered to the skin,
unravelled, brought again to wool,
undone and spun and wound and knit,
unravelled and again.

The day in her possession the ball
trundled through her clouded vault.
Does she look up. Does she consider any more
its crowded threads, its woven durability.

But every time rising to the same routine,
body in the practised bind,
she plods the programmed path to food
to tucked in tended nest to head under wing.

Oh Sister, the big world
is turning round another sun, hadn't you noticed.
And here you are with your old wool gone ragged
and greyed, rolling it monumental, satellite to it.

He betrayed her many years ago.
And before, her mother flipped and threw dance-dress
and shoes in the fire. And she was not only gorgeous
but dutiful and gave of herself and so she was deceived.

Her hand cools to the chipped banister,
dips ungloved in soapy water, reaches
for the old gravy, the same brand of plain flour.
She turns and there he sits. Old Ball. Ravenous.

DOMESTIC SURVIVAL

When skin fails loving, try these:
the tallest winking Christmas tree
a rare Spanish bed
an expensive flatscreen television.

The list will lengthen like generations:
summer holidays planned in December
visits to recognised culture spots
shoes at killing prices.

We bind with such wrappings a cardboard box
in which a severed heart still beats.
Through a single hole a tenacious vein
chains it to its host, damnably true.

Before the Knife

Naked his hands are attentive and his long fingers
fluidly cause commotion.
There's nothing he won't do.
But feeling lapses out of form
when they sit opposite and eat.
She wants the story of her body
to be told in all possible ways
and queries him with every slight saccade.

Time becomes a torn net
intention slips through.
All those shining fish –
who will catch or document their phyla
give a finding of their muscular winnows
across the floor that no light reaches
where they cruelly seem dull?
She pouts her lip and shifts in her seat.
Her eyes sharpen, spark on bitter stone.

He's a worker, has tailored his identity
to the system for the sake of a crust.
Must he also be a raconteur, a clown?
When will she bare her teeth in sweetness?

She knows and wishes culture would dissolve
to let them talk by brain-map only
instead of schoolwise mannerisms
and geographical turns of phrase.
Only grass is required for what lovers do best.
Passion and the gun conspire to wipe empathy
at the hint of bad grammar.

Discernment costs.
There might be no other waters.
For all she knows this is what's given.

In species terms this man is precious
fine as diamonds
just unstrung –
the state before the knife.

KNOWLEDGE

A silent man
guards a closed well
you must approach
naked if at all.
How does he know
what a coat conceals
when so much happens
under every surface
rippled or smooth.

Pushing
the cover off is labour
done in purple stages
like the crushing of grapes.
The reward is rich.
A new exposure calls
the sun to make gems
he'll clothe you in
like a nascent queen.

Caution.
Dark water simmers
in its own gut
and will think nothing
of sucking you down
into its cave of twisted mirrors.
Or hurt by your struggles
sweeping you pebbled
to a turgid sea.

LOVETALK

Lover, when we talk
I might as well drop stones
into a rift too deep for echo.

Lover, in our talk
we cast sticks to a rising volcano
– firefood with a quick hiss.

Lover, as we talk
I could be wielding my blunt Moroccan knife
against the stormy sea off Valencia.

Lover, if we talk
I'll never sleep, because you take up guns
when the mouth opens as if I were a canon against you.

Lover, when we talk
and devices home on the seven openings of my head
I imagine your death.

FAITHFUL

In bed with a man she no longer touches
she dwells on one she does.
She seeks her nipples for need of him
finds them already sprung and hard.
That's how they are when they reach
for a deeper groove in his palms
tugging her skin behind them.
A cat shaping to a caress.
A *touch-me-not* seed pod
exploding at the tip of a finger.

Now that her skin has been re-tuned
it's an instrument faithful to itself
will intrude its specific colours its
random flaws into all melodies.
She makes a space round where she lies
and breathes deeply. Inhaling an absent smell
she sinks herself in it hoping to be invisible.
Exhales only when she hears a sigh
and the resigned beginnings of a snore.

OBSERVATIONS

The velvet month. I hang a bauble on a tree
and watch my face bulge. Years ago I did the same
on a tiny plastic spruce we thought modern.

Once a pauper always kitsch. Tinsel haphazard
as snowflakes or tumblings of the wind; cheap
golden angel though we don't believe.

I used to be handmaid to a man who ate his children.
He swallowed a stone and couldn't spit it out.
It's maybe there yet, anchor to the grave.

On Christmas Eve, being mother
I'd hang a joyless chain of streamers and watch
the house totter in drag, myself as poorly masked.

You can keep childhood. Eighteen was my lucky number.
A day in stupor with *Jameson's* ten-year-old
made Christmas boom with a big bass.

December lights came up on beer-buried counters
homely trysts in the snug of O'Neills, an attentive brother
with last-minute packages from Arnotts.

Old routines have me fussing round the kitchen
in amateur haste, throwing instant icing on a last-minute
cake, muddling mince into husks of pastry.

We light candles and sing half-hearted hymns
to the goddess and her curried stars. Crib incongruous
but the youngest insists it celebrates a child.

The long pretence grows starker by the year
this post-industrial imitation of a life, nothing pressing
but the recidivist wheel of generation.

And then – his face grinning in the hanged trinket
his brother's cheerily cherried by the fire
their opinions on human waste and

the remote behaviour of the otter and the wolf
their eyes gas-burners stories ignite. Pinpoints
of light in these pointless observations.

Quantum Politics

These are politics –
the look between mother and child
the possibility of safe passage from room to room
negotiations that dry tears.

Every day I revise
the tired feminist lesson – that it's all personal
that behaviour informs the rule
that we small ones are blood to the social vein.

Talking to him here in the kitchen
of Barack Obama and the great leap forward
I'm watching his strained shoulders
and thinking of our joyless bed.

If it's more important to me
to hold a penis in the palm of my hand
than to discuss a national election
am I a quark subsumed unobservable?

Politics has been rocked
by the penis-holding palm
the flavour of that dynamic
how such flavour informs the wide web
from particle to wave to wash.

true

you loved me a thousand once.
i'll give you that.
i'll give you this too –
your sweater live in my hand.
a pleasure to inhale
your presence in its fibres.
can i hold you
proxied in your clothes
go to our bed as i used to before sleep failed
and i moved across the landing.
your touch was always silken
and it made me rest.
lay me down, your trappings
stroke me like you did
your breath riding my breath.
forget you're not still that cushion at my back
the willing consoler
the one who stood for the dagger throw
the

AFTER THE BREAK

House heavy as a fallen empire.
Every room has lost morale.
Shadows invade the corners
and wear the foundation.
There was a dream I had before we bought it
of a large room, my sister teaching
and a white maggot army laying siege.
I placed store in dreams then
but still signed the alliance.

History is false to the little
and those raised on the outskirts
with no taste for public life.
Silence was my block
and on that sponge this family house.
Now sinking sideways there are odd smells
despite the Moldovan cleaner.

My sons don't appear to notice.
They stand thoughtful as scholars
about to leave for a city with patronage.
They've heard rumours of a regime
uniting hoards in a solid peace.
There will be no restoration.
Obvious in the wheezing walls.
Fiddlings better burned.

overload

chemicals spill from receptors
neurons suck axons to themselves
    no i'm not sharing
swollen every lone cell
    is hunted by hungry signals
ionised by resistance
    society my tornado
too many effects no meanings
    colours clashing eyes can't
remember yesterday's patterns
    what pulse beats
hurts the chest that stores
    mother not an option
movement improbable
    stillness nowhere
breath not in possession
    hard and fast
identity an ocean stone
    eroding
what remains

climacteric in the extreme

the room darkens   foetal faces draw
   spotlights from the dense matrix   she kneels
not a whimper but centrifugal quake and strain
   ovular potentials huddle in lines for stringing
   crowded and frozen onto a tight choke
she hugs her shoulders   surrogate   unconsoled
   and a creature leaps out trailing chains
   goes surfing the tidal walls
he will not come again to her bucking bounty
   her bawdy talk her raucous primitive yells
   she will not be the bright goddess of the barstool
   fabled and revered in ten parched villages
hail of the ripped legend falls in blades
a thing of flesh flames in the mouth of the monster
and she recalls a hard prophesy told in the spring grass
   lincolns rev on the melting brick
   informants crouch in a lonely copse and beg for mercy
   in the torture room the air sparks and yellows
   black seeps into old pictures
   and the girl with the lank dead hair creeps
   blindly from the screen
she probes her body and finds a silent blowhole
   her fingers return a thousand red messages
   that pool and brindle in the cradle of her palms
if she screams she doesn't know but colours
   curry the weather pumpkin desert and vulva
   lunatic yellow bum-in-the-gutter green
she crashes   glass and glint fling themselves too
   watches her eyes picked to the veined bone
   girl crook and goblet smithered
   on the lizard-dark floor

CUTS

The Colorado artist is a mother, slim once,
still pretty in a dumpy way, midriff swelled
from comfort-eating and the loss of love.
Her face is inquisitive, alert to a world
that has splashed it with waters cooler
than she expected. Her husband never worked,
spent nights shooting up in the sitting-room,
asked her to wear spandex of a sort she baulked at
though possessed of a reasonable nature.

Now he's gone her son and friends do drugs
in the same front-room, while she paints oils
in an attic strewn with hand-made Mexican rugs.
She entertains, makes no secret of her embroilments,
is clever on writing, prides herself as a critic.
Teaches, welcomes collaboration, does multi-media,
lino-cuts for the challenge.
Every picture has a scissors set within its margins
incongruous or not. She doesn't

know why, trusts her instinct on this.
I suggest we all need to put limits
on our stretch, or find ourselves sucked
by other lives, pulled to extremities
of confusion, helpless satellites kissed
by the leggy lips of a spider planet.
She shrugs, says lino-cuts are her best.
Yes, she decides, *definitely my medium*.

ANARCHY

seeks a rubric
>After ten years of marriage he recalls his first
>reluctance, her beautiful face at the altar only
>enough to convince him of genetic thrust.
>Dove-haired children, distaste for scenes,
>constrain him to longing and apparent success.

his bed with a stranger hand each day re-makes

presumes a natural order
>She was convinced of her virtue, devoted her life,
>kept a good house, loved her children.
>Her mind never veered to loose enquiry.
>Their love still died. Her small dam perforating,
>water at her ankles, she sits limp not waiting.

at her window self-absorbed the ash sways

buries the compass
>He is fair to his family, his nobility rooted in
>solid precepts. The ideal, Platonically, is first.
>Humans poor industrial seconds, cheap.
>What choice but to disown his sodomising son?
>If the boy takes drugs it's proof of his decadence.

wild geese arrows skim both

can't hold to the standard
>She has a fire in her that blazes inarticulate,
>only knows her middle-class comfort
>is irrelevant as it is good, her husband too.
>She leaves her young children, lives by the sea.
>Hopes to wrench a name from the flux.

unvoiced the tide advances

This Unmothering Matrix

Embedded in dark
you know what you won't admit.
Tons of silence will eventually drown
the vision and stir
the passion and demurral.
You'll be untraceable
in egoless memory.

So confronted
your chest becomes a prison yard
your blood tells itself dance inner
its ambition   what it learned
from the tall painted sunflower.
Hatchet men are replicating
unseen. The worst kind.

THE CLARITY OF KNIVES

You thought of yourself as the great connector
someone who took stray things
and gave them direction.
Your aim was to weave the race
into one seamless silken cloth
everyone a thread and a weaver.
Nothing you did could strain the fabric.
Nothing should be cut.

Wherever you went silk threads
trailed your movements
snagging on chairs and doors.
It made you feel everywhere at once
and burdened by your life.

Every so often your sister the rebel
would throw a silk scarf in the air
hold a sharp sword under
and let it be sliced as it fell.
No! you'd panic.
Silk is too precious. Every thread is precious.

It appears history didn't agree.

not good

a worm eating from the inside

how it got in is the question
                    and not the question
more urgently how to stop it chewing
                              gnawing
more urgent still how to stop becoming it

in its mouth now and gasping

overhead the cave roof is pressed with vulture-eyes
worse
          eyes of faithful dog
          beseeching cat
          horse you've flayed
          cow you've milked to contraction
they recover
they not you are good

your stomach is undigesting
                    shipwrecks everything
these eyes are not green
they're grey and cloud

you must leave
          cut the rope
          or see it tauter
those threads will not be broken
except in sacrilege

the others you tell yourself
are bound to their own boats
strapped to their masts
you must command yours

shake the rope from your leg
let the stone sit sulking.
step into the room and smile.

As in a lucid dream you focus on your moves.
'Hello,' you say, 'I'm delighted for you.
Congratulations.'

VERIFIED

The truth is a plough.
Especially in the night.
When it expertly slices.
Your prone and helpless landscape.

No-one sees you then.
Bleeding into the murk.
Yielding up seed and groundwater.
Insides mercilessly displayed.

Later all that's visible is the harvest.
Tall and sunlike as maize.
Or squat and struggling – small potatoes.

CORRECTION

I was wrong of course
not to give myself to the proper living
of a green and pleasant life.
The love was there, the hearty neighbours,
teachers guides to high degrees.
My own girlish cheeks a discount.

Indelibly mistaken
to bind myself within a turning cage –
my self my own self my self again.
No bright side encroached on any scene.
I turned each sentence inside out.
Chewed trite philosophies like dried meat.

Was baldly incorrect
in my assessments, hooked on handed images.
Stood neither shoulder-to-shoulder nor alone.
All those abstractions were a curse
when I could have planned a career, played
the market, noted the news.

Self-deceiving.
Armoured with inert paranoia. Found
reasons to be fearful in a fresh leaf.
Thought later it was probably genetic.
Applied psychology could have turned the day.
But I was good at school therefore sane.

Probably mad
not to aim for the current pantheon
thinking kudos nothing more than costume jewels.
But for all that – when one son plays guitar
the other assesses the economy of Africa
I plan a course in consciousness

my muscles tauten to a game of squash
children laugh at my facile jokes
I can smile on most encountered days
and someone yearning in the eyes
takes this, my cage-pocked self, to be admired –
I have to ask of course if I was right.

BREATHING

I'm breathing.
Not living.
Spewed from the bed by habit.
Wonder am I already given to the high winds
such a space hums between me and what they call world.
I don't live as I love
or where brain could breathe
or where smiles rise more readily than shrieks.
Why do I walk this parching ground
pulse drumming the rhythm of an order I can't fathom
gasping from oasis to mirage
lost as the unexamining sky.
In a time of achievement I'm staring out the window
at a shivering tree
working in a two-bit job
putting on a face and the air of success
when I regret every minute of my unimportance
the years spent waiting for life to drop in
the moony pub nights
the drools and delusions I gave energy to.
I fight and get nowhere quick
no hour like the last
no one reflecting because *Where is your face?*
And these love acts with the mechanical substitute
because it's not my time.
Is it ever my time.
But time is manically tapping
knockknocking
jiving at my expense
that unhuman groove sounding
as I inch helpless towards the void.
The dog needs walking.
Another drag.
            Stick the earphones in the iPod.
Hope the battery at least is charged.

Here's the same old limited path
rabbits scurrying from the enemy scent
trees growing up and out who cares.
The last green enclave for miles.
Nature in a nutshell.
    Press a button and a split second says
    with an upbeat drum
    that something is about to shift
    is about to cross
    to the *Bright Side of the Road*.
    Van Morrison can help my feet – I can't –
    or my lightened arms
    or my suddenly fuck-it-all body
    that says by itself
    let those others think what they want
    let them look nervously away
    because what is there to lose
    except this moment in the morning air
    dancing to the only accompaniment
    on the bright side of the dark matter
    on all sides sun
    because
    well because
I'm breathing

BE IT

it reaches you by a tortile route
laying moments like odd-shaped stones
that plot your island.
it is there at Day 1
when only needy simply
you hear VOICES
reaching into your littleness.
HERE they say
(here girl   here now)
is the Definer of YOU.
you repeat Definer of YOU.
No they say Say ME.
ME
(look I did it myself   all by myself).
you must echo because that's the way
(she has a way about her   this is the way
we wash our hands)
HOME. you know. the place with the roof and the love.
so ape mimic or say little. SMILE.

lower
when it speaks it is more like rhythm.
says maybe baby yeah baby
we should be together.
but YONDER the gang
(my gang i wanna be in).
so thinking choice a rubber knife
you kiss and thrust.

Day 2.
Rattling hum.
Pain in the gut
calls Halt.
the gang are in your abdomen brain
(taking you PLACES. all together now).

you *what* in the radius of their eye.
begins a drum beating from the inside
skin bulging to its pulse
(still wants to play though you were untrue).
your heart your lungs must stop
be separate long enough to pick it up
and alter your timing.
will you after all these years
(you never thought you'd meet again)
embrace the uncompassed conundrum
get low to the ground
gather its selves
your stony moments
and be it

BEFORE

It's night in the garden. The scent of jasmine bleeds down
the trees, sick from the day's swollen heat. The skin burns
but cold currents snake from the earth, storm the ankles,
line the long journey of bone that must walk. *Must.*

She's stretched on the ground with a stone in her belly
that fell from a far star, bearing its history. She inhales
and breath snarls to a hammer pounding on the crux
of tomorrow, its mountain, nailing each step and slip.

She knows she will do it. She will push the boulder from
the entrance – over and over – until silence is the scent
and sound of her breath and her rented garden withers
in the gapped memory of the perennial race.

She might kneel but every organ and sub-atomic labourer
says stop, pipes the pomp of ego, sings of limbs glorious
on the inside, their subtlety black-widow treacherous.
You can be, they intone, *the killer and not the dead.*

But there's a place of Bliss, she says and tastes the grass,
*where the generous go. Embrace happens there and fingers
lace themselves artfully and bodies dissolve in the sweet
unity of the right thing. I picture myself at the gate, ticketless.*

She and the jasmine know this and the jasmine will tell
because scent and long fingers make the earth deliver.
She slides onto her stony belly, inclines her knees to fold.
All tomorrows, till sunburst, unwell and inward, *Hello.*

ACT

1

I link to streams of ease.
No one fails here.
Nothing intrudes of the knife and barb.

I recline in a hammock of air.
Swing slow
though skin and hair fly.

Every other pulse is pause.
Room for horizonless.
Seams unknown.

2

Hold then push against the breastbone.
Mime: the rib cage is a whale
a slow moon the heart.

There is no body
only breath and push.
Permeation.

I empty to the outside.
I, perfect as puppies.
Apply.

3

Path is met with far feet.
Huge lungs channel.
Last things are now.

The extra mile will be gone.
No atmosphere impure.
Ignore standers.

There is continuous arrival.
Maps have motives and lay-bys.
Try what is conceived.

4

I am retractable membranous,
hooked on the world's will.
In particular, intent to express through time
what expresses itself.

With every felt event
I unfurl and comply.
Tremors dissolve in allocutive
Act.

STREET MAGIC

*'Magic makes people vulnerable. That's when they're the most
beautiful, because they're no longer hiding and no longer afraid'*
— David Blaine

Live Burial

Every day I settle more deeply into what feels like earth.
I wake to the sinking. One more meditative step down.
I sense a smile from what's below as if I were expected.
There is no silence. Constant chirruping inside the skull.
At my crown, where the window is, hubbub construes
the street and its unsleeping haemocytes. Haridas
swallowed a thirty-foot strip of linen, pulled it through,
sealed his ears and nostrils, made a drawbridge of his cut
tongue and shut down. It will come to this. Why descend
to meet it. The room empties of itself. Grains settle in.
Living is task. David Blaine lay in a glass coffin
beneath a New York pavement. Fame, fortune, fortitude.
I wake because there are eyes, walk because legs.

Vertigo

It will come to this too: the absence of gravity. Accepting
my small perimeter, I rise to each given step. Air thins.
I drain my body of toxic input, open my pores to wind
that takes me for tone. I taste everything. This is not lack.
Simeon the Stylite bound his ribs with palm leaves, went
fasting into a well. Hauled up, he inverted the trip, stood
thirty years on a small square forty-nine feet high.
Survival was not in question so why did I desire. Mind
randomly pushing buttons, or hope for the unseen hand?
Following this narrow path I hardly think of freedom.
I am surrounded by carved cats. David Blaine perched
eighty-three feet above a New York park, a piece of wood
for luck. Belief beggars itself. I circle my paltry ground.

Cold Reading
I do the Tarot. Unbelieving, although a reader in London
troubled me for years. The centre cards reveal the quest
not the querent. One true lover, one kind and careless.
Change, success, later disappointment. My plans shiver
on the wheel. I persuade myself I'm no puppet and shirk
the ominous tide. Where is that high cerebral eyrie.
Chance is no computer, futures quantum possibilities.
Psychics note tendency and type, tell from leading
questions. The secret history demurs. Peering closely he
said, *Where is your husband?* and *You don't give love.* When
it comes is time enough to know life's an impatient bus.
David Blaine reads minds by tricks and statistics.
I slow my breath. Life is a lottery. One can only attempt.

Phoenix
He slides his hand through a jeweller's window, draws
out a gold watch. The couple gasp. Her naked wrist
makes her squeal. My brandy glass traps the screen.
Cradling its golden globe I pour another. Cosmetic
resolve lapsed. I'd rather die than be considered ugly.
'Fuckin' 'ell!' the boyfriend says. She shushes. 'It's TV.'
I lower the glass and slide my hand up my leg. Her face
is close, then Blaine's. Daring little me. Iniquitous by
proxy. But the chemicals flow regardless. Fingers, brandy
and fuelless fire curry up a carol in this warren of lives.
Outside, a fake ogham hopes for heritage – history forged
in red brick nouveau. The room contracts to a single
capsule of real flesh. You win, David. Life is magic.

YOUR GRACE

You are alone in what they would call a new life. What
　　they don't know is that for you nothing is old.
Each morning is a question, as though you were a web
　　living each day in a different cell of itself, seeking.

Seeking maybe nothing but in that mode, hiatus behind
　　and before. It has seemed true to take a sable cloth
to the slate of fact and not only wipe but cover, occlusion
　　of the frame removing the form entirely.

Entirely it might seem, but like minerals that leave a trace
　　in water, small events make change.
Tonight you remember a Columbian dress you bought
　　on impulse at a Fairtrade sale, undyed, handwoven.

Woven into your consciousness now like most of your
　　clothes, but you wore this slinky to a wedding
and people remarked. For the first time you thought your
　　body taut and normal, not a flop. You flaunted.

Flaunting was your wont in a sub-chador sort of way.
　　Exclusivity the bait, the prospect of private vice.
But you see in the mirror tonight a shape that could turn
　　heads. A Grecian curve at the base of your back.

Back to you sitting huddled in a lone hut by a struggling
　　fire, watching the small yellow flame fight the red.
You had blocked up each gap of the hedge. Beyond, how
　　could you know several had gathered to your grace.

Grace was a false thing you said, being rustic. But many
　　thought you walked like a careless queen.
They took the switch in your hand for a sceptre, wielded
　　fiercely against the meek, shaken at the indifferent.

Indifferently endowed you thought you were, and
        hardly cared, but for the faint sense of an untried trail.
It occurs to you now that you could have kept your own
        counsel, sat straight-backed and been petal-showered.

Showering in what was given you might have made
        plans, not waited for a suitor to tear at the hedge
and tell you your mind.

NAKED

*[Contemplation is] 'an utterly impersonal awareness of the essence of
the thing observed.'* – Christmas Humphreys

Look
how naked things are. Whether it is
    a drop of water that shivers on a leaf before its
    inevitable spatter
    the small red throat of a bird aching for a mothering
    morsel
    or a hand that discovers for the first time the softness
    of a face
the world is always exposed.

But we don't always see
even when the extraordinary stands before us.
    No more than we see the true colours of the sun
    that are naked as trees and speckled birds.
This proves that exposure is not the key to sight.
What opens the eye is its relation to what is present.

When I say you're beautiful I take in
    the shape of your face
    your classic nose
    your woodgrained eyes
but not just.
There are times when with nameless clarity
streams in you marble
and by a tilt of the head show history.

What I see then is more naked than form
more tangible than flesh.
In that sight your skin is clothing
    and when it casts off
    you're still there
an event luminous and unforgettable.

Weather has no memory. From hurricane to snow landscapes and moods merge into one unreflecting moment.

Weather is not sorry. Leaving cities in shards it breezes to the next event with a billionaire scatter of self.

Weather's actions are its body – limbs of lightning thunder-stomach puffed raindown cheeks ice-white airskin.

Weather talks to no therapist despite its complex. It has no idea who it is. It never gives up the ghost.

ANY OLD GIANT

Too many of my family, like God, have died.
Deserters in times of need.
Praying knock-kneed is not now my habit
but like all life I seek the unconditional.

The generation's conditions are numerous:
style, manner, possession, performance.
Candid conversation and psychology lack feet
to reach the liminal at the graveyard hour.

Rising then on the pre-frontal horizon
the acned child of only a lecherous demi-.
I hope I am not my thoughts
and fall into any old giant embrace.

your lips

your lips were needy for something practical.
but that's dreams.
i drove you home.
that's dreams too.
your lips sucked me towards you always.
i was for you
– even when i couldn't admit it –
stuck on those soft flesh ridges.
wanting to – so to – fall.

we had
– you'd have called it sex –
signals happening between us.
but you blinked and i gollumed.
froze the curling wave.
hoarded the slide of your fingers
and the desert peaks of your breasts.

your lips by which words were formed like
– let's say – pearls
were not precious except to me who
wore them for the downthere feel
the allover buzz.
i meant it when i asked you to bed.
you said you'd dreamed us doing it and laughed.
that's when i knew how others feel for once.
you tease.

now we're estranged your face still crops.
were you a true – *well* – love?
whether or not – no regrets. because this
– your lips –
was not to be missed.

space

wide open

your fingers searching past midnight
tease the event horizon
     part gaseous swirls
     think worlds
     whose light can't reach you

explore now and ever
it will not be the same
     those rogue strands of inter-planetary matter
     will remember you
     will tauten when next you approach
a smile of intent will be enough
when you are entangled
the way will weaken its resistance
slow its dark walk and listen
flexible walls heaving
what there is will be given
     and still light eludes

your fingers want to be longer
how much must you travel
             study
             experiment
to know this world
your brain itself unknown
therefore your instruments
and this space
     that is cave
     has no end
even when with greater calculation
     you boldly go
     and are swept in

you're absorbed
and glean more data
phenomena startle you with feeling
        here a sound
        a sense of water
        a flat shape bulging to satellite

the hope is unity
        finding and the found together
        collapse time

instruments evolve
the world replies
        tells you things without grammar
        explains itself in signals
you can't wait to decode

BALLET

Because he doesn't dance
but his eyes follow the cavorting of birds
and, dwelling on that grace, he circles inward
plotting the pattern on a closed grid –
he must often take a woman in his arms
and believe his fingers send her dreaming
of a flying ballet leap.

He's made by music
but his voice fails it, and his walk. Duty calls
and leadens the outside, so he moves stiffly
from task to task, an armoured car stuffed with flowers.
Serious as Beethoven, as bewilderingly light.

Where her melody knots he releases it.
Hands of science then art.
He churns her butter back to milk
as the iron around him heats and blows
throws the whole hard history of its regime
into an exquisite terrifying molten pirouette.

CROSSING

In these intimate border crossings
pores and porousness collude.
Your tongue on my swelling petals
mine on your straining stem
delve deeper like snakes to a hidden home.
Everything remains, forgotten or not
and these hours in the candled room
are changing pathways.

Tomorrow when I walk it will be your oiling
that loosens me, your breath at my spine.
The mouths you fed will be my smile.
These shudderings, your aftershocks, my cape.
Subtly by silent concordat
your territory reaches into mine with loamy fingers
sifting resistance. Until like a flag
something proud and colourful is raised
above the blurred lines.

like

i like you lik-
ing me in the afternoon
when you throw off your shep-
herd's skin and go rammish in the lawn cot-
ton blind laths on your back for stripes.

you like me lik-
ing you at 4 in the day wearing nothing
but fingers of sun egg-
y allover and the yelps of children kite-
ing between the houses.
they'd need to come close up to see
through the venetian so it's alright.

put an eye in the pane anyhow.
make the lashes slowly shut-
ter and the pupil post-drug.
make it that big-world-eye storing trillions of image-
s like ☺
        the polish family at their meal of fish and rice
        watching futurama
        the big african husband filling out
        a small job application
        telling the boys to kindly be-
        have.
        then there's this window and inside
        a pink freckled woman is sleeping
        with a story of long tongues in her head
        and pressing backup against the kitchen sink.

so we're not really special but together and that's as
good. so i want you to like allome and at the same time
allothose too who in the afternoon like some-
thing maybe even them-
selves.

CALL ME SWEETHEART

When he called her Sweetheart
did she flush hidden
and did her vagina think back
and remember incendiary fingers –
yes whose –
among the folds and creases.
She looked down, diminutive as she was
then faraway as she could
in the small green world of the post office.

And he of the premature belly
the video-game eyes and the
I've been to Orlando t-shirt
had this matter-of-fact way.
He carried on queuing and observing
while she waited patiently in her neat red coat
hands in a loose elegant clasp
never wavering from what was nothing
to everyone else.

Little woman creased as an overwashed slip
you think, must do, of your first
boyfriend, rarely the best
and then the one who altered the vista
made you think you were Audrey Hepburn
and could have anyone
 – line them up, you'd say no –
but in came the children and their tornado.
Sucked into them weren't you, all gobbled up.

Now in the more or less still aftermath
this not unattractive
young fella has to open his mouth –
his I-do-D.I.Y. mouth, his I-like-kissing mouth –
and bring it all back.

When what you wanted to do today
was buy a stamp at the minimum price
stick it straight in that nice neat upper right-hand corner
and post an official letter.

PART II

YELLOW WOMAN
Eclogue of sorts

The Seeker:
The movement was small and quick, caught from my high
glazed window, stolen from the glare of the urban
pastiche. There was a flash of something yellow beyond
the buildings, like a fox crossing a dark road, but the shape
was a woman's. Then a frozen moment, as though a single
raindrop had stopped to be noticed in the pattering mob. I
found myself chasing it, her. This was the place but where
is she?

> *Yellow Woman:*
> *in a green hedge masquerading as a small sun*
> *see me sway see my petals spread*
> *welcome welcome to my yellow bed*
> *my soft thrown sheets my yellow furry pillow*
> *and my stem that takes you places under all this rain*

The Seeker:
I don't understand this landscape. It's lush in places, then
sparse in vegetation, then sandy. As though the ground
were breeding its own weather. And what can be eaten
here? I see no sign of farming.

> *Yellow Woman:*
> *in the fruity eateries at the tops of trees*
> *watch how my tongue slinks about*
> *peeled priapic bananas*
> *licks pineapple*
> *sucks kiwi and bulbing ripe tomatoes*
> *showers you in juices after all those clouds*

The Seeker:
My clothes cling to me like frightened children. The
pursuit has made me sweat. I let my jacket fall. Then

everything else. It's warm enough to be naked but for how long?

Yellow Woman:
skin cling tight in a flimsy wrap
is cloaked by trail-web clasped by shell
dress green in grass and purple in heather
with a flared skirt so my legs can stretch
and your head sneak under after all that noise

The Seeker:
I have commitments. I have a duty to the race. Urgent messages, admonishing bleeps, a tin chorus of efficient routines, make the score that colours my life. Here it's all indolence. Nothing seems employed except in swaying and sending smells.

Yellow Woman:
my femurs feeling through confused grass
i twist shake limbs learn the melodies of small
make them echo make them echo through
hear them gained always by another
whistle them to you after all that wind

The Seeker:
If I didn't worry, if I sank and spread my limbs,
would my mind become that dreaded thing –
an obsolete machine pitched in an empty room,
thoroughly recycled, never knowing what it has become?

Yellow Woman:
everything has value in the nether parts of trees
gorse tangled bushes stray thorns
i am currency to every rush and riverbank

hold shares in breath and wide spaces
give you ground for yourself after all those quakes

The Seeker:
The ground has spawned a fluid feel
as though it were it about to fly.
Back to that tin chorus, those needy bleeps,
a callipered symphony.
Or simply
fold me in

The Boat

He lay foetal in his own internal drum. Prodigious but
    an anxious student, he had always hunted
the principles that rule the world. What after? Lie awake
    when it was high time to be asleep
and let the screws of knowledge blitz his unsheltered
    ground. If that, then what, then where
to go with which kind of step. He loved her and she gave
    sound support, the bared breast
incitement to prowess. That he was her hero stunned
    him, a man of no sporting force, muscle
only mental and aggression nervous when it came. His
    honour was complete and then dejection
as all that learning unapplied sank without record in the
    grey pool of daily Civil Service.

He of all people knew it was neuronal, but he believed in
    the stubborn resistance of will.
Fought physical diktats, smoked himself bronchial. Liked
    whiskey to a worrying degree –
it only kept him restless and daggered by cramps, which
    he never told and forgot each night
when he grittily proved his endurance and style,
    knew the names and vintages of wine.
Living was test – of his intellect, his lovability, his reason,
    his wit, his weight in any currency,
the faculty despite his depth to be good craic, a decent
    man. He had made a suit of mail
for himself link by link and now he gleamed, exceeding
    the substandard childhood.

He believed in the transubstantiation of genesis. His
    father was in him and he in his father.
Tradition was a cloak he took blue as royalty. It was a
    means of loving what couldn't be helped

and proving, yes again, the value of the given world. He
    learned the songs and poems, spoke
something like him, took his side, made a myth and
    heaved the sacred sword. Had home.
She slept justly and he tried not to move. His forehead
    rippled with a wrangling of worms.
The squirming hoards argued, grew teeth, and he knew
    the truth of every dragon tale, unrescued
princess and bluebeard's museum of heads. His eyes
    gouged themselves to graves.

He was a closed and buried coffin, the principle of
    delirium, the phrase lost forever, the lack
at the sulphurous heart of everything believed.
    Imploding his fingers turned against
him, thinking by themselves to reach over and throttle
    her – why his love? – no, him.
Claw at that head and eyes from which at any moment
    now a monster might burst and leave
him shelled, please, oblivious then at least. And as he
    was at his least he went pleading
for something else, because he had become nothing in the
    face of what turned. Stirrings
happened round him; a scene from the late conversations
    with his father – a boat.

Here was the coxswain, his uncle, long before the navvy
    he became and the cave-dull flat
in Kilburn. Laughing, his father too, young men as yet
    unhounded by the body's rationale.
The water wobbled and crooned. Hidden sirens rolled it
    on their backs, playing fair for once.
He sat small and clearfaced, basking in his elders, their
    endowing love, as they bantered

and erased more future with each cast of line. His back
    eased, fingers unclawed, first principles
found unsolid substance and smiled. Life was a wave
    and not undoing glue. Wood wafted
into sun. The happiest day of his life, his father had said.
    Unfurling he sailed

shaman through the hours until the sky turned saffron.
    They looked at it and knew they had to sing –
old songs of the great bewilderment, their chests buoyed
    with all they could never have described
in any other way. At the end they all cried, and when the
    moon came down she found them
clung to each other, a new creature of many limbs that
    said nothing but shed itself lakeward,
fluidly becoming what it was before. He came up
    convulsing, knew it was the water cure
that soaked his pillow and fountained into his mouth.
    Carefully he dabbed his cheek respectable
and looked towards her dawning eye. She clouded for a
    second, then smally smiled.
He too.

THE CONFESSION
(A Murder Poem)

Bound to happen she supposed, this crime,
in a place so amorally green, still wild,
meadows flourishing however paths
patrolled, set to tame the careless.
Tangled hedges hid weasels and rats,
badgers because they turned up dead.
A Sunday park for parades of kindred,
gentle mothers and the viable young,
glazed assumptions of harmony flipped
to cider parties and rape, confounded her.

He was a horror of a man, she'd heard.
The town knew pornography stuffed
every corner of his murky home,
stoking his feel for the flesh of boys.
She had two sons and driven mad
by early motherhood, suspected every
sports trainer and smarming priest,
felt naked to predators, blooded, unhinged.
Bulletins fuelled her fears with proof,
unearthed weekly some odious offence.

The wrangle inside her of hero and villain
bucked and champed in the domestic bind
but was only itself, altered nothing.
One night, well-tanked, she tore from the house
and staggered cruxed to the glooming park.
Morsel of moondark, fearless like snakes,
the ravel her mind. She ventured desperate
through tangled places. Found him in a sullen
bend of the river, drunk, half-conscious,
holding his cock, crooning like a satyr.

The plot was set. She stepped and pushed.
He rolled resistless off the silent bank.
The flow was high from recent floods –
a sign, a congruent natural caprice.
Looking in, she mused *Why live?*
Convention answered. *Suicide is history,*
no child's legacy. Salvage the possible.
Her chest calmed. She surprised herself
by going home and making love,
then measured her days in tolerable cups.

Loosened from anger by delible time,
thirty years later she wakes in a sweat,
a woman of sixty, hefted by recall.
She's been guiltless, no crime suspected,
but now her youth stands accused.
Was it the same she? Was it the whiskey
possessed her then, ousted her will?
Her husband sleeps, cherished now
that complex survival has topped love.
Contrition leaps from her in tongues.

I had no right, none, to eliminate
Another life. And how inhuman
was it to wipe all sense of guilt,
or was forgetfulness a sign of right?
Why the sudden need to be shriven?
Why resurrect so late what was buried?
'Or sunk,' he says, staring at the river.
She's shown him the place and confessed.
He's a silent man, won't tackle depths;
secrets can scratch in their undead tombs.

He skims a stone across the water,
breathes deep and stretches his arms,

rises for home. 'Can't be helped.'
Neither remitted nor retained,
the sin swims among the river's small fish.
She's in sweet horror at the close shave,
a triumph her woken conscience disavows.
Fingering the house-keys she sets her penance:
remain, work hard, be faithful and generous,
cryptic as a caterpillar, never fully to commune.

PART III

the end of august

1

vatic, you or the season have brought back
frescoed days in which i beam as though
the big questions were ease. repetition rules.
pay attention to the solar ritual and i meet
an old theme, but this time i hold on,
letting the proposition gather and grow hard.

i know nothing.
with this knowledge i see a one-eyed orange cat
who looks at me like baal and mouths a feline thought.
i know no-one. an immigrant passes en route to work.
he wears a neat rucksack on a neat bike.
his retail uniform matches his smile.
i imagine a girlfriend in a neat house.

i suppose this same is better.
the sun plays a shadow fugue on the reticent houses.
knowall.

2

the man unlocking the school gate
reminds me of a mouse
with his round shoulders and bowed head.
a mouse voiding the cat's eye will make itself
humble as a gateman.
its sides will hug themselves
and it will draw in its head.
the dead spit of nothing.
look, nothing at all.

mice are big with us this week
since you, the triumphal human,

found yourself liking one.
the huddle, the black eyes.

maybe the gateman is scared
of great economic cats.
i see him holed-up and watchful.
his mother in the house.
her clone the wife.
their creaking blinkered bed.

3

i reckon you're taking what you can.
i'm a fantasy folded in your neat bag.
when prime commitments are tidied away
doll-i becomes your plaything.

not that i want you beside me always
but i carry doll-you as an action i must plan.

i brake at a traffic-light and tell myself to cast you
from the closed circle of this thought. But
your smell gathers at north windscreen
and scurries down my stomach
to the argument of pleasure.

4

i talk.
you readjust like a camera with a new owner.
unsure of the method, you mine for opinions.
they lie flaccid when you leave.
hastily chosen presents.

5

you lift the coverlet and i creep in like a lonely child
shrinking myself tiny to be safe and unseen upon
the soft mushroom stalk. i settle my head under
the roofing gills of your eyebrows.
your arms and i are putty, become a soft pulse
in a large singular vein.

6

no matter what we've said
mornings keep sliding onto my skin
bright-eyed as your hands   those silver snakes
that nest within themselves
disguised as tongues.

7

your laugh is a cloak.
then it's a weapon.
you're toughly civilised and expect the same.
too free to construe, you have forgotten yourself.
i don't need you.
slam the door and walk away.
return because i doubt my premise, which must be true.
as you prove,
sitting with whom you do not comprehend.

8

you clutch. i'm a restless bird
straining to spread wings.
your fingers probe through feathers
to the skin.
i lapse into something prior.
amphibian.

9

i read your letters and see you dissolve in a brooded sea.
you rise again as immiscible disks of colour that spread
into broad strokes for the kinder emotions.
this is your loving and the way of your fortified mind.
who in particular do you need?

i'm never with you when you want things done.
i might not praise it any more
than your amorphous state before a new question.
i like nobody so well and am said by this when
your hand
tames me into idling time. there is never enough.

10

you'll remark on the curdled leaves and think
of counting them.
certainly the trees.
your way of seizing the day.
i muse into shopping for a new dress.
you'll admire and i'll pretend a spotlight.

this candle we've lit is a show for the few eyes,
glimmering the side altar.
though bright enough if it's rapture you want –
by the perfectly unreliable body
by eyes that can link coital
by skins that pull each other tight
by all that waits in the quarter of a million species
undercovered by the sea.

the second of april

history
I walk
    Home is in repeated kisses of foot and ground
I am having affairs
    With the pavement – for one – complicit as a riverslice
I glide on ice
    tiptoe on the unreflecting glass panel of a foyer floor
Nakedness is rare
    I don't tell how I used to mesh my toes with sand
But even that was a skim
    I slyly stepped on a rock and – recalcitrant – took off
I pause at running water
    Its inscrutable fingers take sun to rock in a work of art
then abandon it dissatisfied
    Among a tree I'm a stretch of soil and burnt grass
and harden
    There are always tears seeming to come from outside
They wash me down until like ivy
    I am again rambling
On a tarred path my jaw is jolted by inexplicable haste
    My ankles wound each other
I bleed and wonder if I should spancel myself to slow
    There are creatures who only pace the one field
Even a hobbled route finds knowledge
    I look at my feet and don't know them
Too long with eyes on a far goal has cost me my body
    Happenings are always outside – strange
when I see no walls   Where is the place of occurrence
    I thought life was movement
Coming to gravel I lose ground and think of release
    Water is too deep and I fear high places
To walk is the freest I can do
    I wipe my tracks
What will pass is the breeze of a small body – non-native
    a light touch on a puzzled cheek

*

on my morning walk
half-listening to wagner
i pause and look up
a surprise of white faces
a cherry tree in blossom

*

the tree
I suppose it's a minor thing –
a small tree with a temporary bloom

its lone modesty close to the shops
opposite the school, beside the church.

For two hundred marches past
I've missed its hammerhead silence.

Now look at me, ghost in the keep
of its pocket, locked to its side.

I curve my neck to the splay of petals
feel a sternum at my backbone

and think how islands know their nature
by their closeness to land.

Is this mindless presence a gift –
this white song, soon a requiem.

Like a phantom ship there's little in me
besides routine and regret.

Who knows their risen sap will lead to pain.
Sin and singing take the same road.

Who goes the journey redacting
might never return, decoy door

to decoy. Name number nation
lost to the maw of a high wave.

*

reverse into dock
white flags bedeck the harbour
the colour of home

*

monotony
Whether it's the world or I draw back
I can't tell. My head can't distinguish
first cause. All I know is all that clings
is a long low tone of horn. It bores through
all things and I see them all the same.

*

ambition
He achieves
a lover, a house, a car.
His special topics are
rock music and how countries should be run.
One for the road, one for the children.
His neurons know nothing
but the stoking
of a driving fire.

*

risk

The Tokyo Electric Power Company, Incorporated, is an
electric utility servicing Japan's Kantō region, Yamanashi
Prefecture, and the eastern portion of Shizuoka Prefecture.
On the twenty-eight of February 2011, TEPCO submitted a
report to the Japanese Nuclear and Industrial Safety
Agency, admitting that the company had previously
submitted fake inspection and repair reports. The report
revealed that TEPCO failed to inspect more than 30
technical components of the six reactors, including power
boards for the reactor's temperature control valves, as well
as components of cooling systems such as water pump
motors and emergency power diesel generators.

Online News Report

*

attention

For all my walking I have hardly travelled,
like a young horse circling a pole.
So what's Japan to me, or Wagner,
but subtle slides on a background track.
We have children, you tell me at dinner,
who need things – iPods, iPhones, laptops;
above all education and cars.
I'm senseless in the fiction of myself.
Write and rewrite. Write and rewrite.
Scrap.

I've never learned how to gaze
and so have missed ten thousand things
that stood before me loyal as soldiers.
A wand is the wave of a thinking hand

but I, I bustle. Will I stop
before I die   before I die.

We start in belief on the rolling tide
and hardly anchor, though we shrink
to a pale ship with an undead crew.
Take a slow breath   become a wind.
Inside things have their own course.
Pay attention.
This is the meaning of change.
Of magic.

*

fury
I fight. Struggle is life.
  What rises freely is hardly the point –
  just a car out of gear, handbrake off.
'Come in,' they chirrup kindly,
  'here is shelter.' I sit and scout the faces
  that bring me cake and tea. They grin.
Empathy entails heart-flop and boneless hands.
  I will not serve.
I know the words and if not boss I will be guru.
  They listen and think I am self
  but I am only behaviour.
There's one I don't convince.
Clarified eyes. Sizzle.
  'What do you mean?' she says.
  'Where were you while the rest of us
  learned a new way of being human?'
Searching for a pokémon I find my pocket
  weighted with ash.

I need a captain and am said by him.
    He declares my enemies.
    I'll never be short of shooting targets.
Turned towards the wall he says,
    'I can't do the social niceties.'
    My tongue and throat let out their water
    and strike a low dark note.
    Respond. Say it. Turn.
If it's truth I fight for
    why not speak regardless of what answers.
    Can I think only in the mind of another.
I refuse a pillow
    and take instead the littered floor
    amid the tarantellic quarks
    ten bottles of *Bud* lined up.
Soldier in a time of peace,
    existing only as disengaged,
    I thin for the lack of savage fare.
    He thinks me strong
    when all I am is a clinging burr
    and he an accidental nemesis
    in this ruleless pointless small war.

*

it has a wide cap
like a lone african thorn
an artless postcard

*

Snake Island
It's not butter but I spread it on both sides, the better
to slide away.
Here I am in my cave, a hoarding creature –
my clothes my unclear eyes my tidy nooks my tomes.

'I *want* to live alone,' I told her, and she went thoughtful.
Look now at the luminous spiders in those nooks.
I have brought her with me.
And Her. And Her. And Him. And Him.
And day on night on day these doppelgängers
work their busy webs.

If I told my sins to your frozen grey gymnast of a bark,
you could harp them where you liked. The one truth
is that fact worms into earth and reappears unlike itself.
Only sometimes among ten thousand things does earth
megaphonically object and claim its judgement.
We gape then at gate-crashing chaos, the huge-throated
killing white *no*.

Bless me Tree for I have sinned.
I made my babies cry.
I made my sister cry.
I made my lovers cry.
I made believe I loved.
(I make believe I'm sorry, thinking of Joni Mitchell.)

Say I can leave my watch
that I can drink with them
wear a new white dress
my stains on the ground unnamed.

*

Total Silence

*

bubble in a teacup
Hush. Confession must stop somewhere.
No absolution is a total scrub.

But I can't ignore the clutter underbed,
the torn cushions, the spilled paint, the broken glass.
Even last evening when he kissed me
the quiver of his spotted skin made me think of frogs.
I stroked his sweating face and turned my thoughts to
other buttocks, smooth as lenses.

It's a manky world, says the tree, *accept.*
Confess all you like but when you walk away
with your sights on a clear horizon
I'll only be a slender hiss at your perimeter.
All that healthy reading and these starry moments
– you know this – fail before the soulless morning
and your sole ownership of nothing.

*

who planted you here
hermit among pruned clusters
stranger to commerce

*

disaster
On 11 March 2011 an earthquake categorised as 9.0 Mw on
the moment magnitude scale occurred at 14:46 Japan
Standard Time off the northeast coast of Japan. Units 4, 5
and 6 had been shut down prior to the earthquake for
planned maintenance. The remaining reactors were shut
down automatically after the earthquake, and the
remaining decay heat of the fuel was being cooled with
power from emergency generators. The subsequent
destructive tsunami with waves of up to 14 meters (the
reactors were designed to handle up to 6 meters) disabled
emergency generators required to cool the reactors. Over
the following three weeks there was evidence of partial

nuclear meltdowns in Units 1, 2 and 3: visible explosions, suspected to be caused by hydrogen gas, in Units 1 and 3; a suspected explosion in Unit 2, that may have damaged the primary containment vessel; and a possible uncovering of the Units 1, 3 and 4 spent fuel pools. Radiation releases caused large evacuations, concern about food and water supplies, and treatment of nuclear workers.

Online News Report

*

The Stillness at the Back of Buildings
This job may look like another of the billion grains
but it's my airship. There's no measuring what buoys
inside when the body is a mountain full of sea.

I sit alone in the canteen and stare at the rear of the hotel.
Grey roof, arched windows, blue frames
show not a movement. The building might be long
abandoned and done by Hopper, the scene flat as a caw.
Not a sound from the rented rooms, not a flap
teasing the glass dome above the dance floor,
the gap between inside and out.

A man in a luminous jacket walks across the roof.
He's looking for something.
This consciousness might as well be in him.
Would there be substance then.
We're flies, the wall cornea-coterminous.
To think oneself big enough to know better
is to shiver at the gable-end. I want my bed.
Let my bones coil nautilus, pre-history.
I've misread every glyph.

*

fugue
You could maybe learn a new language if you
understood your first.

'Isn't that drink delicious?'
'Delishus.'
'Who's good? Isn't it nice to have a treat after drama?'
'Ure gud. Snice to have a treet.'

The expectant mother coats every gesture in chat.
In thirty years' time, the child will sit in another café
recalling the hot chocolate topped with clouds of Mammy
cream, chocked with Mammy mallows, and the words will
be hieratic. They will rise like necessary bread and be the
stomach he marches on, the credulous brace of his
shoulders.

*

where does the routeless girl
find her summer laughter
you think she's a sun
hot enough to be fused
but she's just a small bird
with a dead mother's plan

*

reap
At around 9:30 am on April 2, 2011, we detected water
containing radiation dose over 1,000 mSv/h in the pit
where power supply cables are stored near the intake
channel of Unit 2. Furthermore, there was a crack of about
20 cm length on the concrete lateral of the pit, from where
the water in the pit was flowing out to the ocean.

The TEPCO Website

*

ken
One eye can do the work of two,
except for covering the other's corner.
The hero's entrance and the killer plane
are equal horns upon a dark perimeter.
It's chiefly context that the pair provides
and still they only see what's in their ken.
Perception rests on hardware in the brain.
To map the field you have to make the fence.

What you've never known won't worry you,
neither will it awe. You bend among
the native corn and set to reap, but blinded
by the sickle and the sway, you forget
the work you do has sense beyond the sense
that, once revealed, has power to possess.

*

he gobbles his food
a boy home from school
he has forgotten
the time between then and now
and his lover's hungry eyes

*

The Dying Pigeon
You blue by the path
thick-feathered subdued
small hatcher unmoving
not the ghost of a vow.

I tunnelled on a line
too high-wired to idle
constantly apprised
to obviate a coup.

I'd go votive now
if I bowed to a myth
for conclusive closure
of these parted lids.

Let me die to specula
and what they reveal
their steely incisions
their accurate untruths.

Then stare button-eyed
no holy man or hope
unreflected by my life
and my meaningless demise.

*

blooms lost the leaves curl
girls hiding their naked breasts
the offstage actor
has no personality
i stand confused transpiring

*

keel
I folded on the deck behind the helmsman.
Nothing else to do but trust his lizard-cool
to take us up and over every booming wall of wave.
Wall after black wall hit eye-screen and boat-screen
and me, spineless and foetal, mouthing *Mama Mama*,
through each silent retch.

A thousand years ago a group of monks,
and later Vikings, rode here toward the dark island,
braving wave and whale for a god at seven hundred feet.
I would never climb a sheer slope for peace or maim,
however loudly sword or crucifix cried Riches.

I close the borders and exclude the stranger,
focus on the rules of movement and the body's poise.
I seem contained but slow breathing is to tease fingers,
phalanx by phalanx, from the gasping neck of reason
and compose the semblance of a democrat.

This nomad empire, small and so contained,
is hardly worth a moment to the tide, but lizard-like
it alters to confound the odds, mandate or not.
Come love or murder avidly it clings, echoing the meme:
emperor, pauper, defiler and defiled
– all caviar to the palate of the sea.

*

the micro sculptor
stands a nation on a pin
inhale and it's lost
just because you can't see it
doesn't mean it isn't there

*

tears
June 19, 2011: The prefectural government of Iwate
released new data that shows radioactive contamination of
grass exceeds safety standards at a distance of 90 to 125
miles from the damaged Fukushima nuclear power plants.
                                        Online News Report

*

begin
the day broke its orbit & shot into red space
black strings snapped   birds shot from them &
flappered on the spot baulked by cruxing winds
tiles broke their terminal set & clapped owners
to the square kitchen strip   puttied them to chairs
no foot could stir but flipped up rusted catches
kicked over trunks & hookeyed through what popped
the walls collapsed & we harpied on bridges
screamed gritted smoke   spat sleets of spittle
denied source & consequence   shrank to hot elements
knew our limbs long & sharp as hauntings
tequila rose amid feathers flesh & steel
bulbed to a genie & pledged us its wish
hours later edible saucers topped with olives snaked in
later still I passed close to your knee & plopped there
long tongues plaited & wound   small dark explosions
haloed our tense pre-morphing pieces   on floor & bed
ships ploughed through storms   thrust   reversed
blew horns   raised sails   lowered them
picasso and dali witched on the air like dancers
crowned us deities in all compass points of the head

suddenly tableau and transparency
eyes opened to clearly nothing
mind as i knew it gone
a flat white plain without crop or devastation
an empty fuselage flew autopilot
olive bough in its mouth
time neither night nor day

A quantum of total silence.

92

Easter 2016

In a house off the Falls Road in 1989, a Buddhist monk
    struck a gong and chanted grace,
a teenage boy sniggered and a nervous tabby nosed the
    saffron folds. The day before,
the memorable sound was gunfire; if there were prayers
    amid the random cracks

they took the veil of air and played dead about the serried
    windows. Buses billowed
into storms of grey complexity from the bombed blazes of
    their guts. Outside the
greengrocer's an old woman braved the shots to re-arrange
    her carrots and cabbage.

2016. Boroimhe Estate. I rise to the small sun sent from the
    obstructed horizon
that casts a gold aura on the tall chimneyless buildings.
    Three-bedroomed duplexes
ride apartments. It's a much-sought-after area. No fires
    need solid fuel.

Meet my neighbours, Krzystov and Rebecca. We trust each
    other with mail. A scent
of bergamot meets you when you call to deliver. Behind
    you the pristine grass is bare.
Yes, I own the orange Persian; she's not a stray. She just sits on
    the wrong mat.

Sound insulation is close to perfect. At night you might as
    well be in Connemara, or
back in Ború's time, in a monk's hut refitted with constant
    light, vaguely sensing
the standing stone on the manmade mound in the centre of
    the closed cluster. Bovale

know how to do heritage: Dal Riada, Torcaill, Milesian
    Court, Coill Dubh. Lest we forgo.
The management is efficient. Litter is spiked daily by a
    brown-skinned man who smiles
at his work. The red brick keeps its colour. Cosy if
    crowded. A maze of content.

I was greener than grass in a Lisburn chipper when I
    linked a Protestant dyke
and asked for fish in my republican tones. Two good
    reasons to die. She knew.
She was always scrambling through the windows of
    married women, breached

the barrier on the Donegall Road to court a Fenian with a
    carved black cat.
I knew a Catholic artist who drew King Billy for UVF
    prisoners in Crumlin Road.
It wasn't religion then, or when the IRA whipped his son
    for sniffing glue.

I did nothing except live a while on the front line, my baby
    oblivious to the casual
slant of a soldier's gun and shootings outside the Rock Bar.
    We scurried back south.
Everywhere is north of somewhere. On a quiet beach I
    wondered how to bear peace.

I heard of sex between militants in an occupied house.
    Death is sexy, she told.
But later, when the red has faded from the cloth, there you
    are with a white sheet,
like too much light. You seek the face and it's white you
    find, the features ironed out –

the white of silence, of carved stones, of women on Xanax,
   of optimistic tree-
interrupted streets, crystalline shopping meccas, scrubbed
   hotels in the cultural quarter.
Flags are too flat for what they support. The miniature
   gardens of Boroimhe take me

back to Rockmore Road. Lay a patio if you can't maintain
   the grass. Later upgrade.
The sage *Persian* hides for hours among the stunted shrubs,
   thinking them a jungle.
You can learn to live anywhere, she purrs, having
   mounted the last wall of the estate

and returned. The boy with the bag of glue spent too long
   on the corner. When his
parents split, he wasn't quite there when he cast a noose
   over his head for whiteness.
These times I recall my grand-uncle, distant as the moon,
   member of the Cork Brigade.

There's nothing so coherent we can say it's done, even if
   we never knew it, though new
shops, cut into the field, redraw the mental map in days.
      There's a greenish lane reminds
me of country behind Airside Industrial Estate. Past the
   fancy Nursing Home, keep on

to the dead end. Like a country road, there are daisies and
   snowdrops. The last house
protests its privacy. And no, 'Boroimhe' is not pronounced
   'Ború', but his corpse was
waked in the now Protestant church, the night after the
   battle, white as a martial suit.

PART IV

LOCKDOWN DIARY
12 March 2020 – 30 April 2020

Day 1

(Travelling from Monaghan to Dublin)

fallacious, the sky muds –
interesting boom to the cable-stayed
bridge of celebrations just passed.
imagine that human. imagine many
expert ladies' maids anchored
to the ends of its long steel laces
and the torso upright as law.

passed kavanagh's memory place
without turning off. manly
type of feminine poetry flavour.
you don't elude the given ground
you re-hunt it. sanitiser
in the passenger seat. hah.
somehow already in the house.

girl in the classroom blew her nose.
girl beside her uncapped her gel
a heartbeat after. do not use hands
for friendly. you are in fact what
last you touched. here comes time
outside of tabulation. how will
you manage weeks without a hand.

applegreen never so empty.
food counters even at freshii
are dull. an attendant gazes nowhere.
there's everywhere to sit. it's not a day
for cracking jokes breaking bread.
plastic gloves are not worn
by the manager who cleanses after.

out in the country somewhere people
always knowing are tending self-
grown basics and still not arriving
for coffee 'n donuts. inside muddy
organs pretend not to breathe.
block flight. shutter the limbs.
curtains twitch. house private.

DAY 2

(Swords Village)

in the window of the lord mayor's pub
a bluish painting of revellers.
remember. you will do this again.

morning bright and even-tempered.
airside low in cars. everything open
but shy. tesco has nothing behind signs
for toilet paper. no peppers no pasta.

do you send children out to play do
you keep them in. man in the pet store
listening to the laptop radio. minute
by minute there might be changes.

the day turns around. by evening
the air is churning again. wind set
against movement. whirring at the ears.
the shrunken world a covered dish.

america in the mode of action. will it
take eight weeks. how to make life
of this place. harvard scientist affirms
self-isolation. we have never seen
this before. we have no immunity.

Day 3

not revellers painted in the pub window
but figures with no faces. look like corpses.
man with white hair and beard playing bodhrán.
man with a pint beside him. white splotches
for features. it is of course not ominous.

nothing ever happens like death until it does.
it's not death it's long inconvenience and some
death. three men together on the footpath
can't get two metres away. they don't care.
four cars on the long road beside supervalu.

dunnes stores on the rathbeale road has run
out of *tfnn* jellies, party mix and mini eggs.
easter is around the corner. large eggs seem
laughable. sit around and gorge. don't tell
head aches because it's ached like this before.
eyes burning. everything wanting to close.

they're offering surgical masks in the shop
that sells phones beside the barber's. seems
extreme. what would people say. hours
later looks like a good idea. follow the isolation
instinct the strict distance. it worked in china.
two months ago i had sex with a stranger.

Day 4

the virus is not pretty but interesting. meet
and deceive. befriend and conquer. how human
is it anyway. protein rules the world. memory
is protein. so are armies. here is their structure
prepared for eyes. like spaceships. two worlds
rogue to each other. do they know who we are.

walking the beach air of airiness. light throw
of a stick. mad race of a dog. dog bounding
virus bounding. same dislocated shock.
the way to get a latté is from a machine. wear
plastic gloves make no skin contact. it's cool
to untouch. it's called social distancing.

not disorder. who comes to visit must sit
far away as the depth of the average grave.
tesco has cheaper bread. again no peppers.
no gel to hand. a masked man leaves aldi laden.
how would you know a carrier from carrion.
is it part madness. will we embrace better not.

DAY 5

morning beams through the small
windows. it doesn't know. inform it.

one hundred and forty thousand
people are out of work from today.

notify the pavement. who will it serve.
do not phone your gp without symptoms.

anything lacking must be got now.
necessity is debatable. idiot. lifetime of waste.

tesco has peppers. make pizzas. freeze them.
since when has food concerned me.

used to break it down to essentials. used to think
a pill would be fine. no fuss. before i knew style.

wandering the shelves three weeks in mind.
you have enough. stop. dredge up some instinct.

look at no-one. quickly pass. it's your duty.
plastic gloves. disinfect them too. aloe vera

and tea-tree oil you can't get them. card declined.
you discover a limit to contactless. only just found

out how much you pay for each transaction. idiot.
after this learn what's necessary. the wind rises.

will it ever stop these dispassionate afternoon attacks.
are we its playthings. how does it want us to move.

flesh is messy. androids are germless. machinic
drive-throughs. robots for waiters. seems like a plan.

six bewildered americans walk slowly seriously on
the opposite pavement to the premier inn. what is there

to see. get the swords express to town. eat where you can.
be merry. james galway's classical style irish melodies

are playing on lyric fm. oh yes tomorrow. wear green.

DAY 6

When at our best we can think with our flesh.
I think singers do it. I think Daughter do it.
André Breton suggested we try it.

There are three chambers we can imagine.
Unknown; Pre-known; Spoken. Like a heartbeat.
Which to live in. Can you dare to forget. What's death.

Homotrimers of S proteins compose the spikes
on the viral surface,
guiding the link to host receptors.

I would like to say I respect your industry.
I think of you as an army of workers travelling
to your great enterprise by underground rail.

You have found tracks in air. (So they exist.)
We are idiots who plod to work ignoring
the huge bustle of Fact, our distant Host.

In the lab real workers analyse the plot,
predict the denouement, storyboard us.
Littleness, anything, is loveable, even yours.

The Airside Starbucks is lightless. McDonald's
drive-thru is backed up. Down by Tesco, Costa
has a sign saying *Now Open*. It is. And empty.

DAY 7

Culture of Containment

What I'm afraid of nightly when I check the locks
is very like the alien entity whose systems understand

but do not care. What I'm afraid of with my dental
insurance is the contingency of ugliness and pain.

It has happened. A hard fall for no reason on a bright
morning. The new insurance is physical withholding.

Everyone keeps a two-metre gap in the post office
queue. The government office wants hard copy

in a period heavy of scanners and wary of touch.
They think a signature must be sealed by flesh.

A family practices social distancing as they walk.
It's almost a dance, slowly advancing, holding place.

We might grow to like this. Top of Main Street
the shoe repair shop is open for business. Small,

squat, a hundred years old, it resists evolution.
Endurance in this case a sign of its own principle.

Insomnia has upturned the chairs on its tables.
Costa and O'Brien's are serving. Like an animal

on hunting ground I want to escape the Pavilions,
the carelessly seated at the open tables and the woman

rushing through with her scarf held over her mouth.
Face lined, body bony. I wonder about the future of sex.

Day 8

Isolation is not exclusion.
There is no sense of a thing

happening to which one would
never be given a ticket. Glamour

is drained of its matter. Home
displaces it. Four walls become

palisade and swelling lake. Gleam
of the virtual closing in. As promised.

When I think of walking it's the sea
or many fields. When I walk it's

where the absence will show itself,
among shops and coffee locations.

Animals of the economy adapting.
Jaws twist from the unsavoury,

hooves scrape at idle soil. No-one
bites the diseased bark. Still, Airside

car-park is half-full, where Currys'
staff will now only serve you at the door.

Costa, Starbucks and McDonalds
are open for takeaway only.

The thing about living that dogs me
is no-one actually does it in the open.

DAY 9

heard. in head. best colonists
adapt native culture to theirs.

arrive with a marriage proposal.
remould the existing coercion.

i'm no colonist. marriage of no
consequence. feel the shape of me

instead. backing in. there is no change
of air. nothing to come to. grip. greet.

you believe it is you. the ground. you.
it is world. i am the prompt. darkly.

of the big picture.

DAY 10

the immortals walk the white halls in their robes of
sky cloth crowns of cloud. what remains is their will.
who their shining hands bless revive. there is one way
of living called breath – what is plainly desired.
another is industry in one's own interest. down
in the rubble. scrambling for repetition. hound
what intrudes. harbour spikes of light to pretend
normality. hang on the moving animal. look what
do you see. threads of you spreading exponentially.
many among many. what does it mean to be here.
account for your still moment. how from earliest days
you were rambling in a room of images without a
quest. while beyond they were delving differently.
arranging for your pretty foot the paths. clearing
the broken glass. mending the tears because they
occurred. you in the business are what – random cell.
stir in the stew. strand in the mane. what small eyes
you've got. holding your thimble of beauty.
your tuneful spot.

DAY 11

1

Dis-infection is life. Intelligence in a small room.
She made us presentable by keeping us clean.
Scouring is a social skill. Then sociality arrives
in the skin and we are expected to slide. For sake
of a laughing god. People present exalted as part
of what you love to name it. [Who was the necrose
to begin with. Your familiar your faithful your friend.]

2

It's annoying to stand in a taped square.
He stretches a foot beyond it and stamps.
So his presence is felt. A sudden hand
on the shoulder makes one jump.
An assistant has forgotten when she is.

What sense does it make to store
plastic lids behind the counter. Perhaps
accidental handling by unclean hands
is a greater danger than bumps
by baristas. The soya latté is delicious.

Chorizo and salami and many more
kinds of meat. An array of rolls, baps,
several types of cheese. *We still handle
cash but contactless, Madam,
preferable please. We're all precious.*

The sea is the thing making a shore.
Such respect it engenders. Happy
it makes us. So reliable we can band
together without fear of a sump
sucking underneath. Don't obsess

about the issues just now, here,
your little one seated in your lap.
Sand is safe. Take spade in hand
and be creative, make a lump
of a castle, whatever pleases.

3

The car park at the beach is fuller than usual at this time.
Everyone always has the same idea. I notice the odd
person thinking of distance behind a slow walker. It feels
like a kind of scattered convention. A woman comes close
enough to breathe on me. I breathe out and pass on, then
wipe my mouth with my sleeve. Why does my tongue
immediately after lick my lips as if it were not me.

Day 12

'It's a wonderful opportunity to go for long walks and catch up on all those things one wants to do for oneself.'

Dublin Fire Brigade tweets: 'Worrying scenes in #Howth today, repeated at other amenity areas across the city and county. The car park is full. Find somewhere else to go, or go home. This leaves no access for emergency services.'

*

To my metal mother, a plea.

Do not desert me now when my whole life has been determined by your gleaming parthenogenesis. It is your purity that has sustained me. Your sweet-smiling glass buildings, your standing steel. Do not close the doors of our home and hoard your love, your shiny love, your exquisite playthings.

I scream outside the railings of the playground. Idle swings. Lonely climbing frames. Things we need to pass the hours you made for us. Our food is your package, our joy your pumped paps.

*

Home is a word easy to pronounce. Unless it's been a while since you talked. In which case the forming of the O absorbs the mouth and you begin to think about the implausibility of H. You search for H in your throat. You try to sound it. Couldn't you forget to close the lips to keep the O in, it's such a globe. How to hold the M that's like the hum of traffic in the morning. And then to let it close into silence when you were beginning to enjoy the feel of your pursing lips.

*

There's almost enough in the small apartment to make me feel in occupation. Now that I can't sit in a café with my laptop I feel relieved of timetable. This is a danger, but I start working as soon as I get to the desk. Working many hours every day. I have a schedule. Work for x hours. Do exercises. Eat. Repeat.

Television shows an IT worker kipping in an unfurnished room with several others, sleeping on a cement floor. Life gets to be a system of comfort versus horror. A continual standing at the glass wall pretending you are in the room.

DAY 13

I knew the Pavilions was winding down and like a pensive knight went there early for the sake of hair colour and *TePe* brushes.

TePe is pronounced same as the tent. Why did they call the company therefore the product that? Nothing butterfly about the Pavilions. Bright for a while then the head asks why the pretence but that's just me.

Bakers + Baristas is the only café open on the ground floor. If I went upstairs I'd see the new glazed link bridge over to Five Guys and Milano and them closed too. Nearer the sky is nearer entrapment in this case.

I hurry to Boots down the winding path noting all the new closures. The staff of Costa are taking their leave maintaining no real distance. Butlers Chocolate Café is open for takeaway only. In Boots I'm offered eye drops as if I'd need them already but maybe I do.

Dealz has the texture of a slump the feel of a hippo. She comes from there with a darker than usual coat and when she meets me beams. 'Good to see you.' Turns back. 'You're looking well.' In my walking gear and peaked cap.

One day in Lidl in a shirt and tie she admired me too. She's round and sweet with a viral smile. Wears fun clothes and fuzzes her hair. Down by the sea I straighten my back for her. We're so different we'd just about do. Maybe June.

*

Palacio de Hielo is a shopping centre in Madrid with an ice rink a health centre a 24-lane bowling alley and 15 cinemas. They've turned the ice rink into a morgue for obvious reasons.

DAY 14

This model has always walked pavements without touch.
A house has never meant much other than windows
and walls that are silent as breathless. The programmed
function is movement through the least resistance.

Watch its self-mastering on the road that does not rise
to meet. The feel is smooth like spring airfeel. Bright-
faced daffodils in many rows recollect *The Vegetarian*,
a novel in which a woman desires the purity of plants.

He paints flowers on her back and she imagines herself
belonged. Something innocent seems to flow in them
because their killings and feasts are bloodless
and their breathing is the deeper meaning of ours.

The difference in the estate is only slight. Recall when
more time was spent here and the question was
what they all did inside all day. The same question
occurs now in the apartment blocks and terraces

where like trained plants or potted flowers we sway
within small spaces and learn that form is a function.
This model does not expect special delights or plot
twists but can surprisingly accommodate them.

*

On the Frida Kahlo calendar March has surrounded her
photograph with very large kitsch red petals. They reach
for her hungrily as only kitsch can.

*

Some people are super-spreaders. To know them is to
contact their virus. What makes them like this is

known only to the virus and possibly the body cells. I find no self-criticisms on the web.

DAY 15

I believe any attempt to bribe a wild boar would
result in death. Soldiers to the core and obscenely
fast, observers say they prefer flesh as a medium
of exchange to a scatter of white stones which
even with orthodontics would never make teeth.

No. If you have pearls, keep them on a string
and wear them close. Especially now when
you are taking special care not to walk the streets
without purpose. Pearls, cool outfits, new coats
have entered a psychic quarantine region. Unless

you are video conferencing or on TV, where
that kind of display still goes on. Round the quiet
housing estate no-one is doing anything for show.
I'm sure several went in pyjamas for a token Big Mac
before the great proxy hunter closed the window.

DAY 16

Day's punctuation. Oral axis.
Scent on the horizon. Fashion item.
Cool hook on the high street.
Social equaliser. Personality clue.

```
                    O
G   R   E   A   T       V
            H A P P E N
            I       R
            N   C
            G O O D
            S   F
                F
                E
                E
```

Oh my Cappuccino, my Promised Land. What strange
flesh-hugging myths have entranced me.

*

The extraordinary artist-weatherwoman on Al Jazeera
announces with her usual flourish that there's a rather
lovely rainbow over Mallorca.

*

I have never noticed so many 'Now Open' signs in
Malahide.

DAY 17

Skin can be brown as wood but never as smooth.
Love to watch the frozen journey of the grain
pretend to move on my elm table and dancing
mirror frame. Mirror like profile, frame like legs.

Skin has its own grains and is it loved. Here's
the trace of its augmentations, experience paths,
crumbs clung to the one spot, leaf-coded memories
made for themselves under boomerang moons.

Forty-five coffins replace the pews in Seriate church,
Bergamo Province, where my niece wants to marry.
They are smoother than skin, gleaming where light hits.
Red decorates the arches and the day sprays in.

*

An Italian mayor is on TV threatening flame-throwers.
Another one is out and about like a vigilante. *A casa!* No
ping-pong on the beach. *A casa!*
A mobile hairdresser, what's that about? *La bara sarà chiusa.*

DAY 18

I often walk through Airside at night.
I like it then. Ryanair's gleaming offices
with their empty chairs and brashly drawn
blinds as if to say this could be you.

This Sunday morning there's the same effect.
A tiny token of cars. The only visible action
the light drifting from one façade to another,
polishing, highlighting, like a watcher.

A walk that used to feel brief seems stretched.
There's no excuse for fatigue. Monotony
maybe drains possibilities, as life in a small
space shrinks your plans, your intellections.

Day 19

Night Walk on Airside
There's nothing here unless you think in multiples.
The shape of TGI Friday's reminds me of sharp-faced
fish. There's nothing to yearn towards, but people
come to these buildings, palmers to shines.

Four red lights, a scatter of yellow. Nothing's
coming in to land. In one of these thousands
of rooms there must be someone who'd eat
the walls, like that woman in England. Truly.

Undercover
To be dropped in requires a certain kind of discipline.
Head down. Learn the native appearance and imitate.
Dissimulation is the old game. Unnoticed in the back
streets and alleys; ducking in and out of doorways.

The best are the ones who only think in straight lines
or pendulums. One cast kills many. One sprint saves
nine. It's a head-down rolling-in movement. Outer
coat camouflaged as the landscape. Moving bushes.

Resistance, Pyrexia
Plane entering bad turbulence.
Your real self your forgotten relations
Rooting for you. Holding the wheel for you.
Throwing switches. Automatons for you.
You are burning up you think, punctured.
Believe. Thousands can fit on the head of a pin.

DAY 20

it is irrepressible.
it causes the arms to clownishly perform.
it listens for the smallest crooked hook.
it lets the stones unturned.
it reaches through muck.
it leaps from the box.
it bounces on the bed.
it almost cries when the room darkens.
it is tied to the tone of the neighbourhood.
it fears stillness more than death.

*

This model never followed its star.
It followed its earthworm   fascinated
by the ugly squiggle down the long tube
    to scrubble and scrim   to rubrub   when
desirous divide all by self to twoself
    slipping off the waistband   letting it
deposited   blindly necessitous wiggling
    away. Crappy days.

*

I think I'd make a very bad military operative. I can't see
mass graves in that satellite picture. No more than I
understand how that other picture showed us what a black
hole really looks like.

Day 21

Walking on the other side of the road means
I don't know the environment. Two overhead
bridges I never noticed before. Does it matter.

Is there inbred self-sufficiency. My mother's long
hours of dark, her cousin's long life alone after
husband-and-pal died, one year into marriage.

To think of a shop is to meet the tensed air of it.
Intercom voice telling you to keep your distance,
leave quickly, handle only what you'll buy.

Currency sneaks between us, a magician's trick;
what happens in the box while the saw gores in.
Trickery, we cry, and adore the smoothness.

*

The map is entirely blue except for four countries:
South Sudan, Yemen, Tajikistan and Turkmenistan.
Four white drops in the ocean.

Senator Cornyn says: 'China is to blame. It's a culture
where people eat bats and snakes and dogs, things
like that.' Swine he forgot to mention.

It's now a war against the 'Chinese 'flu.' Shunt them
on the street, pelt them with banalities like
Go-back-where-you-came-from.
If they're over 80 deny them everything.

The Frida Kahlo calendar page for April poses her
in purple, badly painted, amid a tacky bunch
of plastic flowers. Printed in China.
But the whole world eats her this way.

DAY 22

'Remember you are the frontline.'*

Distancing, manically passing, we tauten the line to slice
the enemy.

The story of Troy has not lost its lustre for the never-
besieged. *Troilus and Cressida* is called a tragic love story.
To understand why, imagine the feel of war.

By day Troilus confronts maces and swords, returns with
his helmet hacked, his shield scored, his horse wounded.
By night he dreams of Cressida, how he might please her,
find a way to be more frequently with her.

Pandarus lays siege to Cressida, devising plans to deliver
his niece to his friend. He becomes a man who makes
women come to men. You would be angry at his
deceptions and manipulations if you didn't remember that
the city has been ten years under attack, cohesion its
survival.

It might as well be the last outpost of breathable air under
a high dome. Within its space of thirty hectares all the
social strictures acting concertedly on each citizen.
Cressida worried about her reputation. Helen hating her
new husband. Helen eventually hated.

The containment pressing every feeling dense as a breast
check. Daily hammering at the walls. Daily risk of every
youth who is not only loved but required, because the
value of a woman is rape.

Cressida is sent to the Greek camp as an exchange hostage
and finally accepts a Greek warrior as her lover. She is
damned for this. She has become the secret flaw

perennially threatening the wall. But for her is it not a necessary shift. *Who owns me now is nearer the top – over which a sheer leap requires arms.*

DAY 23

I'd been contemplating roses.
I learned I don't care for them much.
Except for the scent and the tea, I could
pass by a hundred bunches unbothered.
There's one thing. A deep red like rupture
nothing else seems to own but blood.

Set against white it's a myth from childhood.
A girl enclosed, a raven who bleeds into snow.
The man she will die for has skin like snow,
blood-red cheeks and hair black as the bird.

Growing roses is a complex matter.
The many systematic layers like a labyrinth.
In Kenya their stalks grow especially straight.
They're expertly grown and much sought after.
It caught my eye, the snowy mound of them,
piled by ebony hands upon a rough new epicentre.

DAY 24

There's nothing particular wrong with her skin.
Three of her front teeth have marks on them.
Otherwise she looks like anybody.

She panhandles most of her day on the street.
She also runs some errands. *We do that.*
I presume she works for drug dealers.

When she's earned enough she reads in Starbucks.
She leaves the bulk of her books at the counter.
She has enough to carry.

It's demeaning, taking down your pants in the open.
She understands the restaurant owners
but now she really has nowhere to go.*

*

A woman I know to see has a very straight backbone. She's
fake tanned and started to arrive in our mutual public
places about four years ago. Her face looks like it's been
carved with a fine mirrored blade into a not unpleasant
expression of shock. Her body carries no excess of any
kind. Her clothes love that. They're well-chosen and
always spotless. Faux fur, faux leather, passable-quality
leg wear. She knows how to buy. She's out of a magazine
with the sheen of a page. She arrived beside me in
Starbucks one Saturday afternoon. Sat a metre away and
drank her coffee upright as steel. Every so often made a
small sound as if to confirm something. Stayed two hours
doing nothing but that. Her hair was perfect. I saw her
today between home and the shop. She had a takeaway
cup in one hand, bag of nachos in the other. She wore an
attractive leather jacket and tight jeans, walked with a

bounce and a slight swagger. Same face, same hair, same backbone.

* *Al Jazeera* report, 4 April 2020.

Day 25

We the isolated occupy Elysium.
Its dimensions are equally etheric.
There are many rooms, numerous corridors.
Endless entertainment.

Streets upon streets of glass shutters
veiled by simple cloths the breeze catches.
My sight in them refracts me. Wishes
wind into them and become tide.

Lights rise and sink. Neat steel weaves
through the ways and registers a move.
They are sitting too close in the front seat
but there must be two.

Visibility is dated. Presence here is of
the whole spectrum. Time transcends light
and becomes a long moment. Instruments
will augment the protectors.

Instruments will be hurried in. So we learn
the cartography of bliss. So we can map
the motions of our desires and not tumble
on needless disasters.

Everything here arises by intention. Transports
effortlessly. As many as required. Stay.
It is here. It is all here. Essential workers
have made this. For us. Sit.

Day 26

The cat pauses at the door.
She has brief periods of sympathy
but they are always over-ridden by fear.

There's beauty in a deserted street,
an autistic character was made to say.
Simplicity. An uncontested route.

Would you be a health worker.
Of course. To solve large problems.
To be in the thick. To get to the core.

You conspire with hypo-stimulation.
You continue with the usual task.
Who requires it this moment.

Are you living your capability.
Will this thing alter the questions.
Haven't you asked this before.

*

I am sad for South Sudan. Its one case came from outside.
The vice-president says distance is the only vaccine. There
are four ventilators in the country of eleven million people.
I think I misread. Ireland is far too simple. For any kind of
understanding you must be re-born. I've discovered the
sea is five kilometres from here. There are now just three
white drops in the World Health ocean.

DAY 27

It's an image of Africa in a Covid sea.
The virus gullet in large. Channel not wave
not grain, by which a king might travel.

In which a thing from a distant orbit
could be conveyed for exploration
and adventure. (Ten billion soldiers.)

*

Attractive pink picture. Have they invaded
the design field. If you're to be conquered
would you like the chain to be this pretty.

*

São Tomé and Príncipe is inconceivable landscapes
                              is a tropical hideaway
                              is a path to paradise

is a nation of two islands
is a delightful jungle
is a magnificent Lost World
is a very safe destination
has interesting (if expensive) accommodations
is virtually free of violent crime and rape
has a gripping history

sometimes squatters in the once great mansions
slow decay of historic colonial buildings on broken streets

Read less ↑
© 2020 Lonely Planet

*

As far as they're concerned there is no-body here.
They establish years.

They send out masters and slaves. They rename.
Thomas was the unbeliever.

Amador is a film and a restaurant and several places.
It is the Portuguese for amateur.

Amador is King of the Slaves who in 1575 overran
the island of São Tomé.

Amador is from the Latin to love. It is a wonder
who does that most.

*

São Tomé and Príncipe is not on the World Health
Organisation map that changed its format from red spots
on white to blues on blue at Situation Report 66, 26 March.
The nation have been added to the list with 4 cases.
Transmission is Under Investigation.

DAY 28

the smell of cut grass. scatterings on the path.
a bunch of long-stalked flowers the cutter didn't spare.

daffodils and tulips in clean geometric arrangements.
is it sparseness toward which functional flesh tends.

the proportions of neatness are glaring now the glass
is unlit in the stores. the premier inn appears to grow.

there it is inside, the rural being, for whom the smell
of cut grass is a something. attention. renewal.

next to the pavilions a new estate is a typical efficiency
of ground. beside it an odd small path. semblance

of a wood. no. remnant of a wood. a tangled walk.
thin trees crushed on each other. a child's wildness.

the writer walks in the forest every morning. unthinking.
when she returns home some character begins to gel.

*

There's a row of flags on a balcony across the way. I saw
another flag yesterday. They mean they're fighting for
Ireland. Donald Trump is calling it an evil beast that
Americans will crush. An Garda Síochána can now arrest
us for trying to get close. How would six months in prison
help. Or a fine that you can't pay.

*

'For some months to come.'
   o   om mo   o om

DAY 29

Several rows of health workers stand outside
and applaud us for staying at home. It's no pain.
The supply chains are strong, Supervalu says.
The recorded voice says. It repeats. Do not buy
more than you need. There are customer quotas.

This is not hardship. Hardship is health-working.
They are smiling. A large tear forms in my belly.
We have lowered the reproduction rate of the virus.
We have done well. But restrictions will be in place
for some time yet. Do I mind. I don't know.

Is this a poem.

*

Would you like this view every morning,
says the unrequested image from Windows 10.

I have learned the reason for ambition and thrift.
That when you have to stay home it is comfort.

The Ugandan president shows the nation
how to exercise. Runs up and down

a huge office. Does several press-ups.
In a small room don't run, jump.

*

The Ugandan president's work-out has had 215,000 views
on Twitter. The top comment says what I was thinking:
Try jogging in a one-roomed flat.
Work hard and buy a house, someone tells him.
A helpful contributor suggests jumping. All their
profiles mention God. No one I'm following follows them.

*

A police officer followed two men into Walmart in Wood
River Illinois and asked them to leave. They made a video
of their exit. Their offence was to wear face masks. The
video includes an apology in text from Wood River's Chief
of Police. The incident occurred on 12 March and the
policeman thought there had been an official order that
masks were not to be worn. No-one else in the shop was
wearing one. The Twitter post had thirty-one thousand
views. Almost three times the population of Wood River.
The population of Wood River is 97% white.

DAY 30

When they were kind they said
Just be yourself.

She registered an open door.
It was slim and was not hinged.

When they were cruel they said
nothing and stared.

She stood among them with a tone
in her head playing phrases.

Melodies lingered, spun on stone.
She went on awkwardly, listening.

Her home was a frame without art.
Things were picked up, placed down.

Meals happened correctly. Walls
were painted. Furniture was neat.

Her clothes were washed and folded.
There was functional conversation.

No-one was particularly anything.
They never thought she was odd.

Liberty popped from the Web with
the best way to wear yourself.

She studied the mechanics of vertical.
Made her face perfect, expressionless.

Her work is repetitive. She likes it.
She barely needs to talk.

Days are procedures. Her eyes train
themselves to the frame's other sides.

*

Officially this is Day 41. There will be another three weeks
with minimal movement in an effort to reduce the
reproduction rate to zero. Nothing less (more) is required.

2.8 million free images have been released into the web.

Congratulations! You're using the latest version of Firefox.

Day 31

1

night. not a move. underneath a hidden beat.
many beats. face displays a kind of beauty.
revise. what is beauty. the casement windows.
the red brick. the apparent absence of strain.
amazing how things work beneath appearance.

when we say secret we crave the opposite.
no single process makes this interface.
between a window and a cluster of brick.
between eyes and a system of solid walls.
between systole diastole and a pared moon.

2

to survive each other we create pleasures.
to survive ourselves we contain the desire.
respiration depends on many small things.
do you need chocolate. do you need easter.
there is enough. traitorous to shop. or not.

3

what makes the eyes that pursue in empty rooms.
but they're not eyes. and there are no introverts.
neither are rooms empty. purposes live in.
we know how to abide in the giant pulse.

*

'It's going to disappear ... like a miracle, it will disappear.'
Donald Trump at an African American History Month
reception in the White House Cabinet Room on the
twenty-eighth of February. Today it's news.

*

The US death toll has today exceeded that of Italy.
In Ecuador bodies are being stored in giant refrigerated
containers.

*

We will return. No. We will resume.
Half of the world's population will be in poverty.
I detest news crawlers. They make no single thing matter.

Day 32

1

The wide eyes of the cow seemed to know
she was money. Irises swimming in a snowy
globe, beseeching herd immunity.

Dairy tastes wrong after constant soya.
Swallowed principles when I took to Starbucks
whose saccharine river set me to the teat.

Where does that leave me. Persistently
guilty. Remembered as I woke that Einstein
had no fashion sense. Spartans trained

their children to endure hardship,
take beatings, walk with their eyes down,
hands hidden beneath their cloaks.

If you could govern yourself you could govern
a large city. They are in essence the same.
An aesthetic of existence

meant the regimen of body reflected
in structure the soul. A moderate soul
is beautiful. In a beautiful body supreme.

'Be a hero. Wash your hands.'

2

A group of Nihangs in the Punjab crashed a barrier to a
vegetable market. Confronted by police they drew
swords and one cut off the hand of an assistant-inspector.
India Today describes them as miscreants and calls the
police 'cops.' The newsroom's background image is a viral
sea in blue.

3

The sudden suck of the person into itself
is the great unbearable of transit.

It is transit. Like the casual leaking of meaning
into the mundane air. Nothing

ultimately sensible. Every ending twists a sinew
in the attentive nexus of hope.

And still you break the call too soon. The indifferent
clock is allowed to haul you off.

Accept absence and think on. But a slow decay
seems like a kind of integration.

Years they say before the flesh reduces to bone.
The inside beauty feeding on its host,

boundless movement, free of governance. Seems
ugly but feels living, remaining.

Unlike the shock of fire. Both self and semblance
erased. In fact the ashes are crushed

bone, but who'd rattle them, who will they scare
away or console, what construct.

*

The Sri Lankan government has ordered compulsory
cremation for coronavirus victims.

Day 33

They arrive upright as pistons, form cordons.
They open roads and close them, do not refuse.
They transport clean up and restore. They can
Run three kilometres in twelve minutes
Do forty push-ups or sit-ups in two flat.
They are the hard fact of the physical state.
Mind over mulling. They will handle the truth.

My father was one. He sang marching songs.
Uniform beats cuffed his feet to a hard square
Kinless music. Discipline constant slicing
Of the gentler undulations of movement.
The aide-de-camp at my sister's funeral
Said the same message five times plus click.
Who'd snigger now. That hospital. So quick.

DAY 34

1

your insides dark corridors you know as names.
when you know the name you place what you love.
and what you hate. but a name is not knowledge.
knowledge is a discipline and a practice.

what walks in there while you round in brightness
delivered like magic is nothing like the olive
also delivered or even the word you produce
to flesh your desire. your made object.

others home on details and manage therefore
to set you on the floor. your gift is endurance
and flow. we are all somehow for ourselves
and surpassing location for the link.

2

Chief Superintendent Pat Lordan of the Garda National
Economic Crime Bureau said: 'The purchaser went onto a
website … which he thought was a genuine website of a
genuine company in Spain, but he wasn't on that website
at all.

'He was on a fictitious cloned website, which was not real.
So, despite the fact that he thought he was purchasing
€14.7m worth of face masks, they did not exist on this
website, he was never going to get not even one mask.'

What kind of human thinks about diction and grammar at
a time like this.
What happens when structural grace is not a concern.
What are we trying to preserve.

*

Austria has begun a limited resumption of business.
They're in the mood for summer dresses in Vienna.

DAY 35

It is always from the depths of its impotence that each
power centre draws its power, hence their extreme
maliciousness, and vanity.
  – Gilles Deleuze and Félix Guattari[1]

What you need to do if you want to know everything is go
to independent.co.uk, UK's Largest Quality Digital News
Brand. There is a large selection of video coverage and you
can save your clicking. You get a brief snatch of a press
conference or news report and then it changes to
something else. They're about a minute long so they don't
get boring.

The government of the world begins in ourselves.
  – *Fernando Pessoa*

Donald Trump reminds me of someone's brother or uncle
who's trying to appear like he knows how to unblock your
sink but really he couldn't care less and will soon slip out
to join his cronies in some fancy hotel and make them
laugh at his smutty jokes.

This is not happy talk. Maybe this is happy talk for you,
it's not for me. This is death talk. This is sad.
  – *Donald Trump*

We don't have a king in this country. We don't want a
king.
  – *Andrew Cuomo*

So that's why a quick-disappearing headline on the
Independent website said King Trump.

Politics: a Trojan horse race.
  – *Stanislaw Jerzy Lec*

Stanislaw Jerzy Lec's aphorism is so often quoted that I
can't locate the original text. I've been reading about Helen
of Troy and Sparta. In one account she walked three times
round the Trojan horse, whispering to the Greeks in the
voices of their wives and stirring up their passions.
Towards the end of the *Iliad* she was hated by everyone.
But they had created her. The wanted one.

The president of the United States calls the shots. [The
states] can't do anything without the approval of the
president of the United States.
– Donald Trump (CNN Opinion)

Donald Trump makes everything seem so easy. Like an
only child with a magic set. It doesn't matter if he doesn't
get the tricks right, he'll just bully everyone into
pretending it's a great show.

I have spent the day imagining 400 million dollars and
what that amount of money could buy.

The 10th Amendment states, 'The powers not delegated to
the United States by the Constitution, nor prohibited by it
to the States, are reserved to the States respectively, or to
the people.'
– CNN Opinion

*

Fernando Pessoa helps to explain why i have no interest in
poetry that's going to 'raise my spirits' in 'this difficult
time.' I recognize the syndrome from the first time i met
my older family members and felt inadequate because i
didn't believe in anything and had no unshiftable
opinions. There's a trend among some poetry aficionados

to circulate 'uplifting' material to help us 'get through this together.' The notion of an ideal state is as prevalent as it ever was. I don't want to be uplifted, i want to be informed. I don't want to be down-to-earth either. I want a feeling of flow and the acidity of immediate sensation. I'm dishonest as the next and will vacillate from sympathy to self-protection. I veer from empathising with the problem of hair to self-castigation over not being a helper (while still not helping). At least don't complain when you are being helped and have a comfortable place to sit and walk. I arrive in considered dress to my video meetings hoping admiration will happen. What's life worth without colour. Ask the virus that. Ask why we are so hooked on linking worth to death.

'For any spirit of a scientific bent, seeing more in something than is actually there is actually to see less ... Only poets and philosophers have a practical view of the world since only to them is given the gift of having no illusions. To see clearly is to be unable to act.'[2]

He's wrong about philosophers I think, since arguments may be based on premises that have not been proved. The theory of ideal forms, for example. I suppose he [or the translator] is deliberately contradicting himself by opposing 'practical' to the ability to 'act.' See complexly perhaps. See honestly. 'Sight' here signifying experience-as-a-whole. All stones turned.

NOTES
1   G. Deleuze & F. Guattari, *A Thousand Plateaus: Capitalism and Schizophrenia*, trans Brian Massumi (Continuum, 2012), 249–50.
2   Fernando Pessoa, *The Book of Disquiet*, ed Maria José de Lancastre, trans Margaret Jull Costa (London, Serpent's Tail, 2010), p. 198.

DAY 36

When the daily email from Harvard Medical School
arrives, it's to advertise a course in Caregiving. Timely
help, it says. But it's not help. You have to pay thirty
dollars for it. I thought I was signing up for good health
information but I've signed up for daily ads.

As I do my morning stretches, I watch an Al Jazeera
feature on the leader of *Communists of Russia*, Maxim
Suraykin. Russia does not want a tsar, he says. Ksenia
Sobchak, a presidential candidate in 2018, said that Putin
thinks of himself as a messiah. He believes he is Russia.
Members of IC3PEAK, a techno band that has been
hounded by the police, call his rule an evil empire. The
lead singer says he will have to be cloned. I don't get it.
The interviewer is relaxed and intelligent. He wears casual
clothes and smiles like a friend. How did he get the job.

*

The danger of being proud brings itself to the table
with these. The quiet-spoken expert with the careful
facts. The calm Chief Medical Officer.

To be addressed by physicians who seem accountable.
The abstract colours the feeling. To be part of this.
Call it Irish. Gentle accents. Sense of reason.

Pretend to belong here. Factually, you are here.
You might claim their ambience as a pet claims yours.
It beats the 'cruel virus from a distant land.'

*

The detail is extraordinary. I'm waiting for Deborah Birx to
show a sign of exhaustion but it doesn't happen. A stage

by stage plan for re-opening business in the United States. The president stands with his arms hanging awkwardly, back bent forward. He might be herding cattle. His mouth doesn't know how to hold itself. When he speaks he calls Covid-19 a 'cruel virus from a distant land.' He describes the situation as an all-out military operation, the greatest deployment of US effort since the second world war.

DAY 37

Being alone is not new. I've put myself in a situation of relative isolation for ten years, transited a long stretch of pain and moved into a capability. What I think I mean by this is that I'm now prepared to call it a choice. It might be a choice governed by circumstances or psychic constitution, or the better of several unchosen options, but this organism has opted for it and is responsible for changing it.

There's no happiness in isolation. Happiness is too fluttery. There might be contentment or there might be productivity. If there's no affectionate contact with another human and no close community, happiness isn't the word. That's not to say I'm not ready to smile or laugh; it's to emphasise that I'm always a little strained.

What's different since the amenities and businesses have withdrawn is an added pervasive strain, a chord constantly pressed. What troubles me most is the question of permission. Everything has become a matter of public duty. Any act of rebellion or indulgence seems impossible. But this is inherent as well. I'm capable of going into virtual paroxysms of anxiety over not having turned off the laminator in the office or something said without thought. So there's no qualitative change on the inside, just that the outside has shown its hand.

*

It's true that birdsong seems pervasive.
It occupied the green this morning
as it does during solar eclipse.

You pursue birds when the city fails.
They occupy your vacated self.
You stop holding out for a human.

*

Donald Trump tweeted: Liberate Minnesota; Liberate
Michigan; Liberate Virginia. All states where protesters
have gathered in public to demonstrate against stay-at-
home orders issued by Democratic governors.

DAY 38

I dreamed I worked in a giant warehouse
up to my waist in water. There were hundreds.
The water was the colour of mud. The roof was steel.
The driving imperative gristled to the air.

It was inexplicable and easy to read. Years
conscious to end in a static continuum of
helpless acts of pass and shift. The scene
coalesced and pursued. A function of bricks.

Amazon Scout wheels evenly over the pavement.
Delighted customers extol it. Engineers have plans
to make it speak. Cute as a dog with a paper.
Cute as upturned eyes.

Baltimore Warehouse is the size of twenty-eight
football fields. With robotic help the millions of
products are easy to find. Warehouse workers
are called associates. No whip marks.

The company is a nation and a culture. An engineer's
delight. They have taken on one hundred thousand
extra employees. Concede. Jaded Amazon.
Water-bound. Weapons obsolete.

*Despite the cavernous space, the skylit climate is remarkably
comfortable, kept at room temperature year-round.*

DAY 39

I understand the man with the falcon.
The leathered skin, the absolute stillness,
tree-lust clutched to the iris rings.

The pet-lover confounds me.
The language of it. The cuddle-tones.
They are beautiful of course. Unequal
also. How the word always covered
the union but never the compulsion.

She will pivot her life to a large degree
on his care. She will weep when he dies.
She would never eat him. She will also
name and cuten him, make him believe
he is made for a life of containment.

He proves her. He makes her humane.
Something unclothed and above suspicion.
He becomes a topic, the means to a friend.
She *Aw*s his habits, makes a virtue
of retention, schooling to fetch.

*

there will be doors without handles
payments by eye and gesture
robots and drones with UV lights in sanitising mode
they will be efficient and replace our hands
guide us on board   let us know when to walk
we will begin to think of them as ornery pets
they will not lick our hands or nuzzle our shins
they will not respond to sorrows or exhilarations
they will lessen our fear of spending   speed our way
when they falter we will climb their mountain
summon by atavistic ritual the miracle of a real human

Enter the Engineer.[*]

DAY 40

on H.D.'s Helen in Egypt

She takes to the floor with a palinode
and advances backwards.
How can she propose

that a whole war was fought
for the sake of a meeting of two souls.
Man and woman and a standard of human.

Feet following a single track.
Union of the creative principles of each.
Eidolon and symbolon, phantom and partner.

It's a mystery how a section can be lived
but you have done it, do it.
Walking and doing it. Doing it and walking.

How the section can be opened
and no other part.
Or closed to let other parts move.

Gods as large as Isis and Osiris
are daily lived between us, sectioned,
apportioned among our bodies.

I don't understand how knowledge alters
from one avatar to the next
and how something grasped can be lost.

Her woman is always walking.
Purple sandals, white veil.
She is a puzzle.

She is full of words she must unravel.
She makes other words of them
and their meaning shifts

like light's revisions.
Words become keys and doors dissolve.
Names make what she calls love and coalesce.

Names mark our loves
but our loves are swarming on their names
like bees disturbed.

For the union of two souls,
the force of their desire in pursuit
of the flowering of their natures,

for the epitomes Helen and Achilles
to walk together by the mothering sea,
the Greeks devastated Troy.

Or, collapsing cause and effect,
the war propounded the principle
of the two genders.

Union in division, division in union.
Isis, Astarte, Aphrodite, Helen.
Amen, Zeus, Theseus, Achilles.

That you can be woman or man
is a mystery. How a veil descends
on the cells' information.

You arrive with them partly in you.
You are not self-sufficient. Not gender.
Only the inscription of a want.

DAY 41

4Chan

1

'My quarantine is about watching anime porn and
videogames.
Why women don't want to have sex with me?'
'Be honest; would you fuck you? No? Then why would
anyone else?'

2

a name at any rate is a thing that unsticks.
does yours draw to mind the motions of you.
leave it at the threshold with the others
like footwear unsuitable for the floor.

does your motion in here suggest a name.
who has the skill to give one. did you come
for that reason. or do you denote yourself
in terms of absence. swarming in syllables.

3

The 'Liberate' tweets induced them here
to talk of boogaloo. A place of shuffling
and shouldering. Haphazard fragments
of pale thought impersonating sense.

4

I have never seen anime porn before. It's the same as the
flesh kind but with wider eyes.
One caption reads: 'Itadaki! Seieki (UNCENSORED)
ENGLISH VOICES!!!'
I think that means: 'Climax! Semen (PAY PER VIEW)

WOW!!!'
Another caption says: 'Real guy hold's wife while she
fuck's stranger's.'

*

The governor declares that he must do his best for the
people inside the four walls of New Jersey.

Day 42

'If they wilt not observe to do all the words of this law that
are written in this book,' she says, holding it up (the little
blue book), 'that they mayest fear this glorious and fearful
name, THE PEOPLE – then We will make their plagues
wonderful, and the plagues of their seed, and of long
continuance, and sore sicknesses, and of long continuance.

'They will say that they are obeying the orders of their
superiors, but I say unto thee, what was it that was said
after the World War and how was it for those who said it.
Lo, they were hanged by the neck.'
She points to the door whence she has come.
'We have taken the name of the judge and our memories
are long.'
She points over the heads of the rabble.
'If those in yellow garments accost thee, ask of them their
numbers and list them.

'And they shall be left few in number, whereas they were
as the stars of heaven for multitude; because they wouldst
not obey the voice of the PEOPLE.'
'The PEOPLE,' cry the rabble.
'And it shall come to pass, that as the PEOPLE rejoiced
over them to do them good, and to multiply them; so the
PEOPLE will rejoice over them to destroy them, and to
bring them to nought; and they shall be plucked from off
the land whither they goest to possess it.'
'It is Us,' cry the Rabble. 'We have them on the run. We
have them on the run.'

She waits for the chant to subside and declares, 'We are
forming a new Citizen's Army to claim back the land for
the PEOPLE. For the glory of the PEOPLE.'
'The PEOPLE,' they cry. 'The PEOPLE.'

*

I wondered what a 'famine of Biblical proportions' would look like. I wondered if they had more and worse famines then or was it just that the Lord God liked to threaten them. The famines were in fact too numerous to investigate and I found myself at *Deuteronomy* 28. Whereupon I stalled.

*

The Courts Service has said it is 'disappointed and appalled' after around 100 people gathered in close proximity to one another in the Round Hall of Dublin's Four Courts while an adjournment hearing over the Covid-19 laws was taking place today.

– Independent.ie

DAY 43

1

What's running out there –
        eye of red   toe of ivory
        brow bent   ears upbowed
        bristles on the take   tail
        filigreed to the gate
        elbows knuckled down
        ah there   unearth it
        parade the way

2

When you said you are made of thoughts
you said to bring the coals in for the old
old fire, the furnace covered with iron,
and stoke it closed and stay with it, your
hands, your posed fingers learning it.

She learned by the quick slash something
made in the fabric of the synthetic fibre
that large knives have a mind to slide
through sensitised channels like eels.
Stiffened to monsters in small rooms,

they hack at the door she barricades
with a laundry basket, a bin, her body
backed against them. He's mindless
or has a mind to attack. Once his antics
were cute, now they're a bucket of bomb-
based nitroglycerine, his father concludes.

3

The philosopher has made a book from one
hundred days. He praises the new communal

sympathy of governments. Will the absence
of a deeper meaning cause mind to collapse.

DAY 44

He thinks to hunt uncandidly an instant
cure. He enters the shade of a linden tree
between two holly hedges in the bitter
season. Chases sunlight with his eyes,
is blinded by its glinting on a golden
fountain. There appears before him a kind
of vision, mooching, spouting from the lips
a misted motto. He bestirs and starts
to chase it but he's heavy muscled, weighted
with a sluggish comprehension. Diamonds
turn his miserly mind. They look such fun,
the mining done in thirty seconds. Pour it
in, the healing light, the bitter potion. Let
me out, the organ cries, piping the wind.

*

Supposing we hit the body with a tremendous – whether
it's ultraviolet or just very powerful light ... supposing you
brought the light inside the body, either through the skin
or some other way.

And then I see the disinfectant where it knocks it out in a
minute – one minute – and is there a way we can do
something like that by injection inside, or almost a
cleaning?

New York Times, 24 April

Day 45

These fingertips bring you by a long circle
here to the presence of me.

I woke this morning with the mind definitely
scattered to the cells.

Panic is an indigenous hazard. It happens
in my idiocy, lone ignorance.

Hauling you then, created other, to my side
to pass the law of continuance.

I want to retire from the pragmatic, turn away
from what is better to know.

With mind in the four limbs, it's not possible.
It becomes our remote monitor.

Moves us and makes nothing of our regressions,
our fancied regressions.

In fact our roundings, these fingertips, have minds
hardly to be called our own.

*

What Ireland's Seismic Network measures
are quarry blasts and the movements of cars.
This is how they'll know if we're a good people.

Apple is less grounded. It will track transgression
by a count of our inadequate travelling sense.
First the roads confound direction. Next commerce.

DAY 46

Fingers and the mustard-yellow sash
create a slim person. Dawn has dipped in.
Walls in yellow attempt to whip
the miser light eking through small panes
into the miser's finer muscle.

Sleek the curtain, flaxen.
Remember the mad seduction
absolute home tremendous death
of the flower azure.

She was frightened to here
by the many moving walls
and must not stay. Every day
she says it knows it.
Knows by shaping the curtains
to a body to a bouquet
smoothing her owns
her flaxen veil, stroking
upward her nippled mounds
downward her belly
rounding her shape
the good passage
link of the world.

It's in the homings
the carefully pouring
forever poising that
she leaps will leap.

Attention does it.
When the body has died
into azure, fingered flaxen
buttered itself on the inside –
up goes the tongue voracious

through the gleaming corridors
perfume on it and colours of slow
meaning –

to lick its good
induce the seneschal teeth, the lips
to bring to the palace the correct
what she, what only she, feels to be fine
not necessarily trumpeted
the sweet-stringent hands.

DAY 47

He's Jim the Dancer, isn't he.
Comes on stage at *Britain's Got Talent*
with his head in a makeshift cardboard clock.
It's a serial act. Last year he came in an alien mask.

So he makes these moves
with no rhythm. Five seconds and he's ushered off.
Next time he's back with four acts in one; he's a cat
he's a boat, he's a disco head. Far as he gets.

Dancer sounds like disaster.
Mulhern gets him to spell it. He goes d-i-s-t-e-r-s-t-e-r.
Does it over again. Mulhern's found a phenomenon.
He can't offend him. Face like a punctured ball.

Puts videos up on YouTube.
With his friend and his friend's money. *Me, I'm poor.*
He sways to Bowie in a shiny suit with a tin foil pack.
They tell him *You're gay, You're a headcase, Keep it up.*

He stalls in mid-move,
has no moves, ever, but his props take time.
500 videos in six years. Compulsive, face covered,
body one string of a web. The costume is the thing.

*

It's a kind of attitude that isn't a million miles off an
attitude I could assume if I let off the vigilance and wasn't
alone so much. I'm referring to the virus deniers. A lot of
people don't understand but it's simple. The only real
thing is what's here now. Your family are here. Your
feelings are here. Your hair is here. The virus is far away
on TV. You can't trust anything from anywhere outside
your four walls and it's annoying when people start

bringing up all those complicated questions. It gives you the feeling that your head is full of tangled rope. You want to get it all in simple language with a clear matter-of-fact timeline. You want your environment to be the same every day and in all directions. You don't get personality or the notion of difference. One World means One Body (yours).

DAY 48

1

You carry a grin with you trying it on everything.
You cast it on the pavement on the traffic light.
Hold it to the door handle and the coffee machine.
Hap-hazard on the walker passing on the cyclist
on the child. Did I mention that it's not *your* grin.
A grin a pastiche of a thing you can't properly
comprehend. Hammocky hold-intent in your mid-
region. Hope it is the hope of an upturn a sink-in.

2

The asteroid is not furry and has no spikes.
It does not replicate.
It means nothing and will pass on the outside.

Does the virus mean that when a hearse passes
everyman will halt
and plumb herself for the absent mourners.

Does it mean our viral metaphors are stored
by Gaia and returned
as the real thing. *We breathe less deeply;*

we have too many neighbours to know them;
we are homed inward;
our conversation refuses depth exploration.

Who does the pronoun mean. The critic
said we are blank watchers
of random happenings. Emptied by them.

When common wisdom comes it's the word love,
arm-in-arm with preservation.
Let down your barriers No raise them Yes.

3

The sparrow of the Williams poem is a poetic
not a natural truth.
Poetry, music, his lusty cry upon riddance of lice.

4

As to how we are discussing the viral topic,
WHO has applied advanced language analytics.
It is the fifth finger in a public health taxonomy:
cause, illness, interventions, treatment, chat.
The analysis is focused on emotions:
denial, sadness, anxiety, fear, anger, acceptance.
Rather than sentiment (positive versus negative).

DAY 49

Phantoms on the street reflect the flipside of space.
      Their gestures drive us back
into meagre castles where delicate walls pretending
      toughness are hung with faces.
The same face repeated as in dictatorships: slightly
      smiling, odd stillness in the eyes.
A moment of identification. It collapses. You examine
      components. Creases and strands
make the territory questionable. Why should they.
      This is not how you are.

What hand props these blank frames that await
      inscription. Over and over you regress
to pose in some imagined context. Pleased enough
      with yourself, statue to some degree sculpted,
presentable picture. As if you were some form of
      currency. A fictional nation comments on
your masquerade. Unforgettable phrases recur and
      oversee your actions.
Moments bulge to your stepping in, distort space. You
      are never the same.

*

Like so many towns and cities, Indore in Madhya Pradesh is traditionally haunted by stories of restless and troubled spirits. And in April its streets were suddenly populated by the living dead, when the authorities adopted ghost costumes to scare people back into their homes.

DAY 50

Gilead

I

A gibbous moon holds to the sky over Airside.
It's said May has arrived, pushed in from a long train
of disturbed tracks.

Rumbling over the time-hump makes something seem
ended. The caravan might rest for the sake of peace
alone in desert space.

Here's what happens along: a squat man wailing at
Hogs and Heifers. The question if he's hurt or vicious
engages but I don't halt.

Cast him in a pit stripped of importance until he can
become given. Turn at Ryanair, led by curiosity,
pass again. Cypher in the void.

He's on the pavement with a rucksack and plastic bags.
He sees me and seethes. Shocks me with a thousand
memory germs of fear and haste

of pounding inside of pounding feet pretending
destination; lion wolf and leopard predators of the
desert; descent into singular loss.

What could he do. Still the body races politically
fast takes itself without looking back
home like a scared hare.

II

In the northern Komi region of Russia
a bishop says to ring the bells.

The bells, he says, will hurry off the Beast
whose crown whose name declares him.

III

I wonder if they had taken your hand and pointed
downward, declaring this the territory – this the track.

In a way they did. But the book of propulsion placed
itself elsewhere, sight unseen, motion made circular.

Out there somewhere is a high place where prophets
find and lay down stones, testaments to pragmatism

called holiness. Oh the survival of us the onward of us
the sacerdotal project masquerading as suicide.

IV

I have made you a fortified city
an iron pillar
and bronze walls against the whole land

Foster City is one of the safest in the United States
with an average of one homicide per decade.
Like the human body it is over fifty percent water.

V

If I left now at 7.15 what dawn
would I arrive at the place of healing.

I would follow your forward-looking statements
your roadmaps. I would find an elevated fertile hub.

I would bend to it. I would wound the bark or myself
for my want. I would suck to consume the invader.

But as usual there is no need to travel. These elements
transcend geography. I may sit and eat my bread

because merchants will come from Gilead laden with
balm and myrrh. And they will pause at my tent.
And there will be silver.

ACKNOWLEDGEMENTS

Some of the poems in this book were previously published in the following journals and anthologies:
'Pale Globe' in *The Stony Thursday Book*, 40th Anniversary Edition, No. 14, Autumn 2015, ed. Mary O'Donnell, Limerick Arts Office; 'Quantum Politics' in *The Stinging Fly*, Issue 13, Volume Two, Summer 2009, ed. Declan Meade; 'Climacteric in the Extreme' in *Orbis*, Spring 2011, ed. Carole Baldock; 'Verified' in *Revival* Poetry Journal, Issue 12, July 2009, ed. Teri Murray; 'Breathing' in *Shine On: Irish Writers for Shine*, ed. Pat Boran, (Dublin, Dedalus Press, 2011); 'Before' in *Crannóg* 25, Autumn 2010; 'Your Grace' in *Dream of a City: An Anthology of Poetry for Limerick City of Culture 2014* (Dublin, Astrolabe Press, 2014); excerpts from 'the second of april' were published in Poetry Ireland's literary pamphlet, *Trumpet*, Issue 7, December 2017, along with a description of the poem's genesis. This poem also featured in the series of events, *cross stream: ways of writing*, curated for Fingal Libraries by Christodoulos Makris in 2015. 'Easter 2016' won the Listowel Writers' Week Single Poem Competition in 2016.

Six poems from *Lockdown Diary* were published in the WRITE Where We Are NOW project, curated by Carol Ann Duffy, at https://www.mmu.ac.uk/write/

Máighréad Medbh has published seven other books of poetry. The most recent, *Parvit of Agelast: a verse fantasy* (Arlen House, 2016), was shortlisted for The Pigott Poetry Prize in 2017. She has also written a prose work, *Savage Solitude: Reflections of a Reluctant Loner* (Dedalus, 2013). Her work has appeared in many anthologies and features in several academic works. Máighréad is widely known as one of Ireland's first performance poets of the 1990s renascence. From the start she has aimed at a kind of consciousness-rhythm that she is always revising and attempting to make more true or more interesting. She is currently pursuing a creative-critical PhD at DCU.
www.maighreadmedbh.ie

Praise for *Parvit of Agelast*

Orwellian, Swiftian in the satiric bite of its allegory, a parable of genetic modification and cosmic meltdown, it is relieved by witty offhand prose asides, it bursts and wrests grammar and language to rise to sophisticated effects … With its bizarre cast and victim heroine it lends itself to a futuristic film or stage drama adaptation.

– Medbh McGuckian

Máighréad Medbh has long been known as an astute, involved and incisive commentator on our world. Here she has made an entire world never before known, 'self-conceiving, self-involved … its own immanent god'. Boundary-breaking even in its form (a fantasy novel in verse) *Parvit of Agelast* is something entirely new …

– Theo Dorgan

… one of the most interesting, original, and arresting works to be published by an Irish poet in recent years … *Parvit of Agelast* gives epic treatment to the themes of gender, the body, time and the meaning of myth in the post-postmodern world … *Parvit of Agelast* is a new kind of Irish allegorical-epic poem that vouchsafes Máighréad Medbh's voice and vision in contemporary poetic culture.

– Philip Coleman